Home Truths

John Peel first presented *Home Truths* in 1998 and he went on to broadcast more than two hundred episodes of the programme. He lived in Suffolk with his wife, Sheila, and their children, plus various dogs and cats, until his death in October 2004. Although Peel's unique personality was always at the heart of *Home Truths*, the programme continued to run with guest presenters until it ended in June 2006.

Home Truths: The Peel Years and Beyond was compiled and edited by Mark McCallum.

Home Truths

The Peel Years and Beyond

Real Stories from British Life
as Heard on BBC Radio 4

Compiled and edited by Mark McCallum

JOHN MURRAY

The ~~BBC logo is a trade mark of the British Broadcasting Corporation~~
~~and is used~~
~~© BBC 1996~~

First published in Great Britain in 2006 by John Murray (Publishers)
An Hachette Livre UK company

First published in paperback in 2007

1

A CIP catalogue record for this title is available from the British Library

ISBN 978-0-7195-2072-3

Typeset in Esprit Book by M Rules

Printed and bound by Clays Ltd, St Ives plc

John Murray policy is to use papers that are natural, renewable and
recyclable products and made from wood grown in sustainable forests.
The logging and manufacturing processes are expected to conform
to the environmental regulations of the country of origin.

John Murray (Publishers)
338 Euston Road
London NW1 3BH

www.johnmurray.co.uk

Contents

The Best of Days, the Worst of Days

Over the years, Home Truths *received a lot of stories from people who, on balance, probably wished they hadn't got up on certain days, or perhaps wished that one day could last for ever. In some cases the experience only affected or scarred the storyteller, but, as you'll see below, a whole cadre of Welsh children had the happy innocence of Christmas brutally stripped from them . . .*

The Giant Fire-Eating Rabbit
Louise Lear-Jones, 2005

From the age of three, Louise Lear-Jones had always wanted to be a fire-eater. So, aged seventeen, she went to the labour exchange to apply for a job in the circus, as you do, and got a job with a group called Circus Sierra. They were a motley collection of different people. There was a lovely Irishman – quite insane, but he loved his horses, and they loved him. Then there was Jenny, with her enormous snake . . .

Louise, meanwhile, was a menial pooh-shoveller who then got a big break standing in for the knife-thrower. She got the job by default, as the knife-thrower had nailed his wife to the board – not fatally, but through the leg. They needed a body.

'Oh, I'll do it,' she said naively.

However, she also got to learn fire-eating, which she'd always wanted to do, as well as swallowing swords, which was quite disgusting. You spend all your time learning to lose your gag reflex, which basically means you hide behind the stable tent where no one can see you putting blunt instruments down your neck until you stop throwing up.

'I met a man who swallowed neon tubes as well. They used to shine. You know when you shine a torch on your hand as a child, and you're absolutely mesmerised because you can see the bones? Well, he produced the same effect but with ribs.' Which was gross.

But Louise wrote to *Home Truths* because of a particular incident one Christmas, when she was dressed up in a bunny suit.

'We were parked up one winter in South Wales. And the thing that the circus did was to pick a different charity each season and support that, and they got a percentage of the take. Someone thought it would be a great idea if we got one of the lorries and made it into a Santa's Grotto and took it up to the Sunday market. So we did. We decorated the wagon – it had a fireplace – it was glorious. We scrounged half a roll of wallpaper, put a photograph of Rudolph up on the mantelpiece, and got an old clock, an easy chair and a rug. We actually made a nice job of it and took it up to the market manager and said, "What do you think? Can we?" And he said, "Oh, OK then. But we've already got a Santa."'

Well, they'd already seen the Santa, and he didn't move about – he just stayed in the one place. 'So the market manager said, "If you want to take the other end of the market – it was an L-shaped market – if you keep to that leg of the L then you've got half and he's got half and you won't annoy anybody." So we said, "that's fine."'

Dave, a lovely clown, played Santa – he was just the right person for the role. And it was OK for him: he had a nice easy chair by the fake fire, and was resplendent in a wonderful recycled-red-velvet-curtain Santa suit. And the clowns were fine: they were covered up and could wear warm clothes underneath. And the ringmistress had black velvet trousers and looked svelte and elegant and glamorous. But Louise had sequins and fishnets, which is not a good look in a market in December in South Wales – or frankly anywhere. So, she wore the only available costume left in the costume van, which was . . .

A huge, soft-sculptured pink rabbit. It had a giant head with floppy ears, and huge overstuffed feet, and big haunches.

'It was like wearing a soft toy. It was massive and incredibly difficult to walk in, but it was warm.'

Louise had the collecting bucket for the children's charity, and she walked – well, waddled – up and down collecting money. She got loads, because the children loved the rabbit.

'Mummy, look at the rabbit!'

'Mummy, can I stroke the bunny rabbit?'

And they'd all crowd round and stroke the rabbit.

Louise found that she'd waddled up to the limit of their bit of the market and she couldn't move for children knotting around her.

'And I looked up and saw the other Santa walking down the market with his robes flapping. And I said in that Mary Poppins way one does when we've got children around us, "Look, children, here comes Santa."'

And Santa stepped towards her and said; 'Sod off, rabbit,' and decked her.

'He'd been completely inanimate. And suddenly he was striding towards me and lifted me off my feet with a single punch to the jaw.'

Santa, it turned out, wasn't entirely sober, so he might not have realized there was a person, let alone a woman, in the suit at all. Like the children, he might have been seeing a giant, pink rabbit.

'It hurt, but not as much as landing on a tray of wet fish as

3

I sailed over the fish stall, which was quite an experience in itself. All I saw through the fluffy, pink V-shape made by these enormous costume feet were angry townsfolk laying into Santa with fists; and Nobby, the owner of the wet-fish stall, vaulting over the remnants of his trays of sole and cod to go and help.'

Santa got a proper hiding. The market security had to come and break up the fight, his beard was off, and children were crying, 'That's not Santa. That's not Father Christmas,' and crying and being led away by angry parents. It was awful.

Back in the 1980s, when some of us had hair on our heads and clothes that still make us cringe, Susan Hicks was a chef, with regular slots on TV and radio, columns in newspapers, and several successful cookbooks to her name.

So far, so Delia. Then there was a house fire, and the threads started to unravel and Susan found herself alone, jobless and homeless. Indeed, it's ten years since she had a home, and in that time Susan has moved a barely credible seventy-two times.

When Home Truths *met her she was in London, flitting between hostels and friends, grabbing floor space where she can. So just how did Susan's comfortable life fall apart?*

Frying Pan to Fire
Susan Hicks, 2004

'It's something that happens to you,' Susan explained. 'I'd become almost imperceptibly of this status – "no fixed address". Which has all sorts of implications, as there are all sorts of things you can't do. You can't borrow a library book. It's hard to register with a doctor. Or voting, for instance.'

But all of this was a long way from Susan's life as a celebrity chef – a term she bridles at. 'A cook, really' is how she describes herself.

She began her career while living at St Agnes on the Scilly Isles. 'I started to teach myself to cook when I was first married. There were so many wonderful ingredients there. I was married to a flower farmer, and we had two wonderful children. We had a wonderful life in so many ways. We had a tied cottage on the farm, and we turned it into a little holiday cottage. And, to cut a long story short, I started a café in the farm shop and gallery that I'd opened there, and was using all the natural, fresh ingredients that grew wild, long before it was fashionable to do that.

'I started to do radio, interviewing local people, and then I started to do *Pebble Mill at One*, going up to Birmingham – and that was great. I used to leave my island by boat, get to the main island, catch the helicopter to Penzance, catch the overnight train to London, and then the train to Birmingham, with my knives, my lobsters, fish stock and everything. I'd do my spot, and nobody was doing fish then and it had a fantastic response.'

This led to celebrity status with book launches, and members of the public instantly recognizing her and stopping her to talk about fish. Then she and Johan, her husband, split up. They agreed she'd live in the cottage, so that they could both be with their children all the time, with the houses separated by just a field. Susan, however, couldn't continue with the shop, so she turned to writing and quickly got published.

When she met a new partner, he came to live with Susan in the cottage. And then they had a big fire.

'We'd spent a considerable amount of money doing it up and were just about to start filming my series *The Fish Course* there and on location around Cornwall, looking at the fishing industry, doing fabulous fish recipes, and using my kitchen as the studio base. And on the very night that the producer was coming over to do the first recce, the cottage burned down.' All they had left was the clothes they were wearing when the fire struck. And they were uninsured.

That was in 1988. Susan and her partner waited a year for the house to be rebuilt, meanwhile camping in the barn, which they put a roof on and began to convert as somewhere to live. But the relationship didn't survive all the stress.

'From that moment on I've been living out of bags and suit-cases,' Susan continues, 'with things in store. I've never actually unpacked everything completely or lived anywhere for any length of time. I did house-sit for friends who were out of the country for four months, which was in the middle of nowhere, and I became extremely depressed there. It was the worst period of my life.

'I tried to make a home for myself in Cornwall, and that was what started a succession of finding somewhere to rent, finding the deposit, starting to rent it – on a six-month short-hold – and then the house being sold and you being given notice to quit. And what people don't understand is when you're given notice to quit you're got to start again the whole stomach-churning process of looking for somewhere else to live that you can afford – and mostly what I could afford was very substandard. Leaky, damp, drafty places. But you were hoping that one could start writing, getting your next project going, moving on to something a little bit more comfortable – with your own choice of curtains even!'

Susan tried finding more mundane work to pay the bills, but discovered in her late fifties that jobs weren't especially easy to find. And low-paid jobs were a treadmill that never get you out of poverty. Moreover, one of her sons is living with her ex-hus-band, and the other has just had two babies of his own, and is moving back to the island. So we were in no position to help.

'The last time I got a notice to quit I was in Penzance, and

I'd been in Cornwall for six months. The mental shutters came down in my mind, and I just thought, "I cannot go on like this. I cannot go on moving." My sons were getting moving-mother fatigue; I was getting moving-mother fatigue. And I decided then that I was going to try and turn my life around and get out of this trap of being in unsatisfactory rented accommodation, and if I was going to be a nomad I might as well be an adventurous and successful one.

'I decided, "Blow this for a game of soldiers, I'm fed up of falling back on housing benefit or asking for help." I thought I'd come up to London and be a successful nomad – fix myself up with a tent and go from archipelago to archipelago, story-telling, cooking, collecting recipes, and earning my way around and writing about it.

'I've stayed in youth hostels, small budget hotels – any-where you can find a cheap room. I went to Heathrow Airport on a couple of occasions, because I'd heard an article on the radio about how the homeless of Singapore go out to the air-port to sleep because it's warm and there's shelter. And I wondered if Heathrow could become the new haunt of the homeless and dispossessed.'

Susan – who looks more like a JP than a homeless person – wasn't moved on, and spotted quite a few people like her. After all, a lot of people sleep over in the airport between late-night arrivals and early-morning departures, so she didn't look particularly suspicious.

Amazingly, perhaps, Susan's sons have no idea about their mother's nomadic existence, and hearing her story on the radio probably came as quite a shock to them.

'Like a lot of mothers, I've been trying not to worry people, trying to turn around that corner and find my feet.'

Chances are her sons and other friends of Susan's will rush around with ideas and offers of assistance once they know about this, but, oddly, perhaps, Susan doesn't really want that.

'However nice people are, the sentence always starts with "why don't you?" as if you haven't tried a million times to do that particular thing. Everyone has been fantastic and supportive – particularly my sons and my family – but there's just such a huge chasm that exists between the haves and the have-nots. I'm taking each day as it comes.

'The most frightening thing is when you really do run out of money, and it's such a sick feeling you really can't explain it. If a payment you've been expecting hasn't gone into the bank, and you really are broke with no reserves, that's really the most awful thing. And you think, "What am I going to do now?"'

A few years ago, Horace and his wife, Clare, became involved in a church with such rigid views that it could be classed as a cult. Horace used to play bass with the group The Specials, *and later with* General Public, *he now teaches at a special-needs school. Clare and Horace explain how they got involved with, and eventually left, the cult which had been so central to their lives . . .*

Leaving a Cult
Horace and Clare, 2000

'We were going to a fairly ordinary local church,' Clare explains. 'Some women there were involved in a very much pro-women movement. They were very dynamic powerful women. They decided to start their own church, and Horace and I gradually left our own church and went over to this one.'

That church took an active role in the community, and struck the couple as both more sincere and more active than the traditional church they had belonged to.

'They were very dynamic,' Horace says, reinforcing the impression the church created. 'And did seem to have a very up-to-date "now" take on the Bible. This made sense for what we wanted at the time. But after a while it seemed to be the Bible mixed with American business-seminar techniques, using a lot of American names – and all of a sudden it was "God wants you rich; God wants you to have prosperity" and everybody started praying for white BMWs!'

'They actually said the reason why people fought over Jesus's clothes when he was on the Cross was because his clothes were designer clothes of the time,' Clare adds.

'There was some mention in the Bible of it being a "seamless garment". It was like the equivalent of Armani or something,' Horace says, bewilderment still evident in his voice.

Horace and Claire had turned to Christianity as an antidote to all the pop madness that had been so much a part of their lives.

'The mistake people make', Clare says, 'is thinking that cults only attract vulnerable people. When you're in these organizations, there's doctors, teachers, lawyers, musicians, artists – all kinds of people. At some level they must feel they have a need for it. But at another level it legitimizes that organization.'

As with all cults, the process of indoctrination was an insidious drip, drip . . .

'You're accepted as you are when you first go, but then there are things you have to change about your appearance, the way you talk and act,' Clare continues.

Perversely, perhaps, one of the first things the church wanted to change about Clare was her hair. 'Well, I had a Number 4 haircut – you know, shaved all over – and I was told I had a demonic spirit of lesbianism because of my haircut. The organization wanted us to change my friends – they called them "cronies". I didn't lose contact with my friends, which was a lifesaver for me, but I did change my attitude towards them. I felt that there was an "us" and "them" situation. Everybody outside the organization isn't "saved", isn't "enlightened".'

Clare's family were also religious, with her mother, sister and brother-in-law joining a group in Scotland – although they've since left. Her father, however, was always suspicious.

The tipping point for Horace and Clare was the cult's focus on healing. 'Absolute travesties were done in the name of God, Jesus, the Bible,' Horace says angrily.

One of Clare's friends had a three-year-old son with terminal cancer. 'I took her to a meeting with a visiting American evangelist – he laid hands on her son and said the boy was well. Fact. The boy had been sent home to die from the hospital – there was nothing more they could do for him. My friend had pinned her last and highest hopes on this, and it was just so painful when her son died about a week later. At the time I believed that it might have helped.'

Surprisingly, perhaps, the cult didn't try to stop them leaving, treating them instead with antipathy. 'The pastor came round and had a talk, and was very disgruntled. If we see any of those people now they look at us with a bemused horror. We're against their organization now, so we're a "tool of the devil",' Clare recounts. 'I have been told I have been possessed by the devil in so many ways . . .'

Horace and Clare joined the cult looking for answers – or maybe one answer – to questions about the direction of their lives, an attitude they now recognize as too absolute and immature.

'We're a lot more balanced about our view on life now,' Horace says. 'We had wanted a specific answer about what we need from life. But there isn't one definite thing. There's a whole series of choices, a whole load of questions.'

'People do generally mature and come out these cults,' Clare explains – 'usually because they're disillusioned in some way. But if people round them have been hostile and unsupportive, then it can be very difficult to find anyone to talk to. It's always important to leave a door open.'

Simon has had a bit of a stormy life so far, but seems to be emerging from this even as we speak. He joined the Metropolitan Police immediately after his A levels in the 1970s, and was in the force for twenty-three years until asked to resign on medical grounds.

Simon's Story
Simon Pinchbeck, 2004

The force has a bit of a macho image, and Simon certainly lived up to it. He played rugby, boxed for the police, and always liked to be in the thick of things – all of which gave him a notoriety and sense of kudos which he then enjoyed but which now, with the benefit of some distance, he realizes was pretty foolish. At the time, moreover, Simon was a father with two young sons, who understandably revered their dad.

'I mean, my boys looked up to me because I was a police officer. But the job had a deeper impact – especially when I did a lot of football-intelligence duty in the eighties, and that sort of work gets under your skin. And I was away from home an awful lot, and I think that did have a detrimental effect on my marriage.'

The football-intelligence work was very dangerous, and after one particularly hazardous operation Simon was diagnosed as suffering from post-traumatic stress disorder.

'It was an incident in the early eighties in a football match between Arsenal and West Ham United at Highbury, and in those days it was terracing and on the North Bank there was a massive fight between the two groups of supporters. But I was found alone between the two supporters in the middle of a massive smoke bomb that was let off, and I was . . . the two sets of supporters were sort of attacking me and . . .'

Simon was the proverbial ham in the sandwich, with no other police officers around him.

'As soon as they saw me in the middle, as soon as they saw the uniform, they both sort of jumped in on top of me and it was a few moments before my colleagues came.'

Understandably, Simon thought he might be killed.

'Yeah, I did at that time, yeah. I mean, I lost my footing at one stage on the terracing, and I knew that if I'd have gone down I would been in real trouble. Yeah.'

Today we would recognize the need for Simon to have counselling, but back in the eighties and in the Police that wasn't the thing to do.

'At that time, with the macho thing in the force, I didn't even recognize it, that I probably needed counselling. I had a young family and I kind of thought if I'd have approached anybody it would have been a sign of weakness. Yeah.'

His not having treatment came back to haunt Simon when, twenty-three years later, he was asked to resign from the force.

'I think I'd suppressed this post-traumatic stress over the years, and when I hit forty I went through a bit of a male menopause and I started going out to clubs and my marriage was looking decidedly weak. I'd left home and I just think it all got on top of me, and I went out one night with a group of colleagues to a club and it just all came out and I ended up hitting – lashing out and hitting – another police officer.'

Simon was suspended for eighteen months, and eventually appeared at the Crown court with the very real prospect of a prison sentence hanging over him.

'But fortunately,' Simon says, 'because of the post-traumatic stress I was able to bring that into play, and through doctors and psychological reports I was acquitted at Crown court and medically discharged from the police force.'

After twenty-three years in the force, the suspension alone felt like a sentence. Although he was suspended on full pay, it was full pay without overtime, and Simon was paying out a large amount towards his legal aid bills. He couldn't work, so he spent increasing amounts of time at the local gym, feeling increasingly bitter and depressed. At the gym, Simon met a new group of people. Unfortunately, they were criminals.

'They were living a life that I'd never really encountered before, you know. They never worked, they always had money in their pockets, they had pretty women around them, they had nice cars, and they were laughing and joking. They didn't live to any rules that I'd been living by for the last twenty-odd years, that's for sure.'

And at that time, in the mental state that Simon was in, their lifestyle seemed sweet. 'It was a lifestyle that I thought at the time I could go along with,' Simon explains. 'Don't forget I'd been abandoned by many of my police friends. Don't get me wrong: I had one or two really good friends who stood by me. But you've got a lot of colleagues, but not many true friends.'

Simon started to work with these men, did a few deals that weren't strictly 'kosher' – as he puts it – and started making money. Even now, he's reticent about the nature of what he did with them.

'I don't want to name specifics, but what it was was putting cash in a pot that these people went off and did whatever they had to do with it and I just gained the benefits from it.'

A bit like an investment really. Of course, if he'd done that in the business community he'd end up in the House of Lords.

Unfortunately he didn't, and the people he was involved with were not the kind it's easy to disentangle yourself from.

'What happened was one particular deal I lost quite a lot of money and I did smell a rat and I thought, "Am I being set up here?" But, because I was enjoying the lifestyle, my greed just said, "Well, hang on". And of course another deal came up and I lost money again. And I just turned round to them and said, "Look, I've got a feeling that I've been had over and I really don't want anything more to do with you."'

It was Simon's wife who helped him dig himself out of the hole he'd climbed into. She got him a job merchandising for a soft-drinks company. This also helped him begin to repair his marriage. Then Simon met another violent criminal down at the gym.

'I met a guy who I knew to be a very violent criminal, and I knew he'd turned his life around through his faith. Funnily enough I saw him in the gym, and my mind was completely mashed – my head was mashed completely – and I said to him, "I'd really like some of what you've got." He said – well, he took me under his wing and said, "Come on, we'll go out to dinner. We'll have a few chats." And he led me to his church, and then came faith in God. And I went on an Alpha course, and I've been running a couple of Alpha courses – just finished one.

'And an interesting point was that, the guy that led me to the church, I used to chase him around on the North Bank at Arsenal – he was an Arsenal football hooligan, and I was a policeman. And when we met and we started discussing that I said, "Do you remember a policeman called the Walrus?" – because that was what my nickname was over there, because I had a great big moustache at the time. And he said, "Yeah, you're the Walrus." And he was talking about all the old times when I used to chase him around the various football grounds.'

Simon's life is far removed from both his time as a cop and his flirtation with crime. But he still feels he has a long way to go, and has to decide what to do with his future. His wife looks on – partly cautious, largely hopeful. His children look on amused.

'I mean, I get the mickey taken out of me quite a lot. But you know that's what happens, I think, because it's not cool to be Christian – especially with their peers – and they think I'm going to sort of start banging a tambourine and hit them over the head with a Bible.'

Simon may have a long, hard slog ahead of him trying to persuade the rest of his family to join him at church, but he's used to this. Life has thrown up a few pretty big hurdles already, and he's got over them. And now he feels better equipped than ever before to deal with the ones in the future.

Peter Davies was a writer with eleven books to his name, critically and commercially successful, and writing his twelfth. Life was good, and to a great degree predictable. Then one night everything changed. A random and ridiculous act of violence made Pete reconsider everything about his life, and the choices he made were startling, to say the least.

Chiller Lad

Pete Davies, 2003

'The first rock came though my living-room window at 3.30 in the morning of Wednesday 8 May last year. It was followed by an open tin of paint, another rock through the dining-room window, and more paint through the second shattered frame as well. Both rooms were trashed. The damage came to

£6,000 – and something like that's going to change your life. You're going to have to deal with it.

'It meant giving up writing. In fifteen years I'd had eleven books published, and all of a sudden it felt like, for all the good it had done me, I might as well have been building a rope ladder to the moon. Book twelve? – I couldn't go on with it. I was in the toils of the justice system, and the Kafkaesque murk of local-government bureaucracy, and there was a criminal thug out there who meant me great malice, so I had to deal with it – and writing books went by the board.

'But what are you going to do, when your life's all changed like that?

'I'd get application forms for the obvious stuff – copywriting this, marketing that – and my heart would sink at the jargon. Then I was in my regular supermarket and I thought, "Well, I like shopping for food, I like cooking it – Why not work here?"

'So now I'm a Coldstore Assistant, Fresh Foods, Band 2. Or, as the job is more properly known, I'm a Chiller Lad.

'There are two of us – one for the night, one for the day. He hands over to me at six or seven in the morning, and between us we deal with the fresh food delivery – which sounds simple enough, except that "the fresh food delivery" is a gigantic daily avalanche. I work in a place, after all, where 33,000 people spend over £1,000,000 a week.

'It takes two or three whole wagons every day to feed them: 2,000 cases on a quiet day, well over 3,000 on a busy one – whole tonnages of ready meals, pasta, soup, sauces, pies, pizza, salads, dips, cooked meats, yogurts, puddings, cream, milk, fats, fruit juice, bulk cheese, fancy cheese, sausage, bacon, fresh meat and fish. All this gear comes through the back door every day in a veritable tsunami of protein.

'As the Chiller Lad on shift, I take this anarchy of stuff and make sense of it. I get it in the coldstore, I sort it, I pick it, I tidy it up and make it ready for the floor – until, over the months, it's become a passion.

'Me and the night lad, we're the keepers of the People's Larder – and, contrary to what some may think about super-markets, I'll tell you it matters to us that everything is clean; it matters to us that it stays in the cold; it matters to us that there should not be any waste.

'So we mash our hands between the rollers crammed against the racking, we wedge our fingers under knuckle-crunching loads of butter and lard, we watch those sell-by dates with gimlet eyes, we keep the code-check file religiously maintained, we sign the Alteration In Price file every day, we stack and condense and rotate our stock with fanatical preci-sion – and any careless body who goes in that chiller and gets messy in there, they're going to get their head bawled off.

'Oh, I'll tell you – sometimes I go on shift and someone's left it disorderly. Ooh – I get the shudders clean down my spine. I go in there and find something's been left scratty, I could scream. I do scream. I bawl. I emit vivid cascades of bluntest Anglo-Saxon. But that's OK. In the chiller, no one can hear you scream. Because the fans on the refrigeration units are too loud.

'But, consider, we have 533 different kinds of cheese. We have 398 kinds of yogurt. You'll need a sense of order to stay on top of that.

'So every day I go in there, and another wagon's on the back door, and fifty-four more roll pallets - each one taller than I am – thunk and clank on to the metal-plated floors of the delivery bay, and I breathe deep and go to it.

'Out the front the good people of West Yorkshire are spilling through the door, loading their trolleys, and the holes start opening up on the shelves down the aisles. I work at a sprint, monitoring traffic with an adrenalin fizz. Cherry-flavour Müllerlight's off sale? Two-pint semi-skimmed is low? Has anyone tidied the eggs up lately?

'So I clear the delivery, I do my best to keep shelves full and folk happy, I tidy up, I file the code check, then I go home and I sleep and I come back and I start again.

'Funny – who'd have thought there could be so many kinds of yogurt in the world? And who'd have thought you could have a relationship with it all?

'But I do.'

Food also plays a central role in Stephen Harding's story. Although here, rather than engendering a feeling of responsibility and respect, as in Pete Davies's case, food – or, to be more precise, that confection of egg whites and sugar known as meringue – takes on the role of dangerous aggressor, lurking ready to waylay its victim. And if that sounds unlikely, read on.

In 1950 Stephen was the Acting Director of the British Council. When his superior was rushed to hospital, Stephen found himself having to deputize for His Britannic Majesty's Consul General at a very posh do . . .

Meringue Phobia!
Stephen Harding, 1999

Stephen was invited to the French consulate to join in the Bastille Day celebrations. They were held in a very elegant Second Empire salon, where he was received by the consul's three very pretty daughters, along with all the other consuls and their ladies.

'I think I was pretty well persuaded by then that I was God's gift to the diplomatic scene,' Stephen remembers.

There was champagne and a tray of bonbons from which, like a complete idiot, Stephen selected a very large meringue – the size of a boxing glove.

At this point the consul brought in his wife for introductions to the company.

'Now, it's difficult to get rid of a meringue,' Stephen says, ruefully. 'There were no plates handy, and it's not something you can give to anybody, really.

'I was in the process of producing a bow in salutation of Madame's hand which would have graced the court of Louis XIV,' he continues, 'with the hand holding the meringue extended in the air, when there was a sound of a small detonation. It was the meringue going off!'

Without realizing it, Stephen had been subjecting it to increasing pressure.

'Hell descended! One of the girls issued a shriek which close-focused the attention of the whole room. I remember removing a large piece of meringue from Madame's coiffure. Her very splendid décolletage was liberally sprinkled with sugar crystals . . .'

The experience has haunted Stephen ever since, although after a decent lapse of time he did feel able to partake of meringue once again. But always strictly in private.

Clive is a successful thirty-eight-year-old, but the experience of being bullied at school is one that colours and haunts his adult life.

The Legacy of Bullies
Clive Frayne, 2000

Clive, the skinny, bright kid with the slightly odd clothes, endured years of bullying at school – both physical and verbal. During Clive's time at junior school, the Frayne family moved every couple of years. At each new school Clive believed things would be different. 'But within weeks of being at a new school, the whole thing would start again, with a group of new people,' he says.

The psychological toll was heavy, and by the time he left school Clive had convinced himself that he was to blame for the abuse. 'I hated myself – I thought I was ugly, not properly male. It was devastating the way it affected my life after I left school. It took me years and years to shake it off.'

For several years after leaving school, Clive resorted to drink and drugs, and found that he fitted in with a group of people for the first time. But at university he developed an interest in fencing and the martial arts, and discovered that he wasn't the uncoordinated weakling he'd felt himself to be at school.

'I sort of overcompensated, with the idea that I could be some sort of Bruce Lee figure. It was rock climbing that helped me most. I always thought I was a coward, but I found I could hang by my fingertips ninety foot up and not be too bothered by that because I was in control. But I wasn't in control round other people. I still find them difficult – particularly other men. For years, walking down the street, I expected to be attacked.'

Having struggled with his fear for years, Clive finally reached the point where he no longer believed that he was likely to be attacked. Then, walking through the village he lives in, he was confronted by six youths.

'I didn't fight back – immediately it happened I was straight back to feeling how I did in the playground, even after all the work I'd done on myself. Although I was probably more than physically capable of dealing with the situation, I didn't. This set off a whole chain of feelings where it was just like being back at school – but this time I could talk to friends about it.'

One of the youths who'd attacked Clive was caught. 'I

picked him out of the police line-up, and just seeing how scared he was allowed me to move on from the attack.'

Clive doesn't feel sorry for himself now, though he does feel sorry for the boy he was.

'It's difficult to talk about – just admitting it happened is almost admitting you're a failure. All my life I've asked myself why I didn't hit someone and sort it out. Why didn't I do something about it. I'm sure the things I did at school were the right things to do to survive. But, emotionally, the question will always sit there.'

Laura Thompson's life has hurled her into a Kafkaesque existence that beggars belief. Normally the word 'Kafkaesque' is overused and misused. But not here.

The Lost Birth Certificate
Laura Thompson, 2004

Laura is an indefatigable, much-loved and frankly petite pillar of strength for her partner, Craig, and their children – twelve-year-old Ella and six-year-old Luke. There's just one basic problem: as far as officialdom is concerned, Laura simply doesn't exist. Twelve years ago she lost her birth certificate, and ever since she has been trying, without success, to get a replacement.

The trouble is that without a birth certificate, as Laura tells us, other official documents and proof of identity are effectively impossible to obtain. She started by listing the advantages of having an official identity and what the acquisition of one would mean for her and Craig's long-term future.

'We've been wanting to get married for what – ten, eleven years? But because I've no birth certificate I can't apply for a marriage licence, a passport or anything really. I've got two children obviously that want to go on holiday, and they've never been able to go on a plane because they don't want to go without mum.'

It seems impossible to imagine that Laura has absolutely no form of identity, and indeed she does have a National Insurance number. Unfortunately that's not enough to get married. Moreover, modern life seems to be actively conspiring to prevent her from getting any more identification.

'Only the other day I had to apply for another driving licence, but right now for the new driving licence – and for everything, apparently – you need a passport or birth certificate.'

And if that wasn't bad enough, when Laura sent her old driving licence off to get the new one the DVLA lost it, and can't find it, so now she has nothing other than her National Insurance number. So, effectively, she doesn't exist – except when it comes to paying taxes. Then she exists perfectly well. You see, her situation *is* Kafkaesque.

Laura takes up the story: 'I was actually going to a chemist with should I say my future mother-in-law if I can get a birth certificate? I was actually in her car, and we went to the chemist and somebody stole my bag out of her car – they smashed the window and took my rucksack. All that was in it was my birth certificate and my work clothes.'

Now at this point the obvious question, hanging, pregnant, in front of us is: why oh why would Laura carry her birth certificate around with her, even allowing for the gross misfortune of having her rucksack stolen in the first place?

'Because of my size. I'm only four foot eleven, so I needed proof of identity on this occasion.'

You see? Another twist in the tale. If Laura had been five foot eleven she wouldn't have needed proof of age at the chemist's. And here's another one. Laura wasn't born in the UK, but at the RAF hospital at Changai in Singapore. And Singapore is now an independent country, and has kept no record of British births.

'I mean, we've sat up until half past two in the morning to phone up Singapore births, deaths and marriages,' Laura says, the memories still fresh. 'We've also phoned a solicitor in Singapore to see if they could help us, and they didn't seem to want to bother either.'

But just a moment. If Laura was born in a military hospital, surely the forces can help? Laura, you sense, has heard these questions more than once in her life.

'I've tried the forces, and apparently my mum and dad didn't register me in Britain. I have a twin sister as well who still has her birth certificate, but she won't let it go to anybody now because obviously she's going to have the same sort of problems as I've had.'

It's as if the fates are laughing at Laura. She has a twin sister, born at the same time, with a birth certificate, and despite all this overwhelming evidence no one will acknowledge that Laura needs to have one. If you made it up, no one would believe you – it's just too incredible.

Naturally, Laura went in search of the registration of her birth, but you can almost guess what happened. 'London's British births and deaths for overseas have got no record of my birth at London.'

Laura's family are as bemused and frustrated as she is. Her twin sister was married in Cyprus ten years ago, and Laura would like to be at the anniversary with her children, and to get married to Craig then.

Four years ago Laura donated a kidney to her twin, and there were no bureaucratic hurdles to jump or problems with proof of identity then. 'No, no there was no problem at all. The only problem that I had is when Linda took very poorly two years ago. Not because I gave Linda the kidney – I was always close to Linda before that – but it was ever so devastating when I couldn't get to her, because I just wanted to get on a plane and go be with her.'

But Laura can't go and visit her. She can give her twin a kidney and pay her taxes, but in every other respect she is invisible. You can imagine how angry she must be with the thief who stole her rucksack.

'I'd probably kiss them now if they'd give it me,' she says, surprisingly perhaps, referring to the sacred birth certificate. In the meantime she has no choice but to carry on fighting for her rights or give in, and Laura doesn't seem the type of woman to give in.

'No, I'm not going to give up – never give up. I've always taught my kids never to give up on anything, and Ella's wanted to go to Disneyland for a long time and I think with the problems that Ella's had throughout her life I think she deserves to go. She's got cerebral palsy, but to look at her you wouldn't think so.'

And it wouldn't be the same without her mum there.

'That's right – she wouldn't go without her mum. But she does absolutely fantastic. We never give up in our family.'

Which is absolutely the spirit she's going to need. But you have to wonder exactly what she can do now. And the answer, sadly, is to go back to square one and lobby the authorities. You can't help feeling that if Prince Harry, for example, had lost his birth certificate he'd not face the ludicrous problems Laura has faced. Mind you, if they find oil in her garden you can bet things will change.

Tom Kelly, a seven-year-old Catholic boy growing up in Glasgow, was training to be an altar boy. It was a beautiful spring day in the 1960s that inspired Tom to play truant from school . . .

Was This the Scariest Day in Tom Kelly's Life?
Tom Kelly, 2005

'I grew up in a part of Glasgow called Springburn,' Tom explains, 'where there was a derelict church that had been hit by a bomb in the war.' He and his friends had gone there to play a game of tag.

Then, suddenly, Tom and his friends heard music – organ music – playing. They turn and look up to the altar. The music is growing ever louder, and there at the altar is a priest – or at least someone dressed as a priest – with flaming red hair. The man is reciting the Mass, in Latin, in a style which even as a seven-year-old Tom recognizes as fire and brimstone. And still the music grows louder. However, what Tom and his friends know for a certainty is – the church has no organ.

Was it the wrath of God?

Tom didn't know, but he did know that he and his little mates were terrified. They ran, hell for leather, across the road to an old Woolworth's store. Just inside was the pick 'n' mix counter.

Now, a lot of impressionable little boys playing truant from school and confronted by the apparition in the church might have assumed that they'd been visited by the wrath of God and seen that as a sign. So what did Tom do?

He went inside the shop and stuck his hand into the jar containing the Raspberry Ruffles – well, they were his favourites. Outside, he and his chums had decided to each try and get something from the pick 'n' mix. He would never have done it if he'd been alone.

Tom had no sooner stuck his mitt in the sweet jar than

another hand grabbed his. Was it the flame-haired priest? No, worse: it was the store manager.

'In here,' he said, dragging Tom into a little side room. 'What do you think you're doing?'

'Nothing, nothing, nothing.' But Tom realized the manager was having none of that. 'He was determined to get me for those five Raspberry Ruffles.'

Five Raspberry Ruffles? In *1967*? That was a hanging offence wasn't it? Now, of course, it would mean an ASBO.

So the police turned up, shaking their heads as they looked down at Tom.

'What's your name?' one of them asked.

'I was determined my mother wouldn't find out what was going on, so I gave my friend's name,' Tom explained.

In fact the police went round to Tom's friend's house, where they found his friend and his friend's furious mother. They returned, very angry. 'Look, if you don't tell us who you are, you're going to end up in jail.'

'So eventually I told them who I was, and they took me to the police station.'

Now you might at this point be forgiven for thinking that for a seven-year-old boy this would be the scariest thing in the world.

No. In fact . . .

'It was OK,' Tom remembers. 'They looked after me – fed me fish and chips and sponge and custard. I was well fed. But they did contact my mother. At the time we lived in these old red, sandstone tenements on the ground floor. And, like a lot of other people, there wasn't much money around, so most of what you paid for you paid up front for, and certainly when it came to gas and electricity and television you paid up front for it through a meter.'

And when people ran low they'd break into the meter. Tom was at pains to point out that he never did anything like that –

his parents did it, thus setting an excellent example for an impressionable young lad.

Consequently, at the point the policeman rang the doorbell to tell Mrs Kelly about Tom's petty pilfering, she was on a stool, on the other side of the door, less than six inches away, getting 'stuck into' (Tom's words, not ours, by the way) the gas meter to get some money out to buy food. And if she opened the door . . .

'We had a friend-and-family whistle, and if you didn't hear the whistle you knew it was somebody else – like the rent man, or somebody looking for money,' Tom adds by way of clarification. 'So he didn't automatically get in.'

What a beatific picture Tom Kelly paints of family life: while he's stealing sweeties, his old mum is jemmying open the gas meter. But, as it turns out, it was a good thing she did, because in those days you needed half a crown to bail your errant child out of the police station.

Tom's mother was taken to the station, and he was brought out of the cells into an office where a sergeant opened a desk draw and pulled out a baton and an old leather strap.

'You can't just get away with it,' the sergeant said. 'I can hit you either with the baton or across the hands with the strap.'

'I'll have the baton,' Tom said.

'Why the baton?' the sergeant asked, somewhat surprised.

'Well, if you hit me with the leather strap I'm going to be in pain for hours. But if you hit me with the baton you'll knock me out, and I'll know nothing more about it until I wake up,' Tom reasoned, with the logic of a seven-year-old – ignoring the potential for brain damage as the huge, shiny, wooden baton crunched into his head.

So the cop hit him with the strap.

And the Raspberry Ruffles? Were they returned to Woolworth's?

No, the police scoffed the lot.

Tom could have gone to school that day. Instead he got

arrested, almost got his mother arrested, and had an encounter either with a lunatic who dragged tape machines and generators around derelict churches or with the Almighty himself. On balance, would he rather have gone to school?

'No.'

In November 1991, Ivor and Pauline Stokle survived an attempted contract killing. Ivor's former wife, Sheila, was the would-be murderer. Her motive was the insurance payout which would come to her after Ivor's death. Sheila, her boyfriend and an accomplice almost succeeded in their grisly mission. All three are now behind bars...

Contract Killers
Ivor and Pauline Stokle, 2000

Ivor and Pauline's nightmare began when Sheila invited them over to smooth out what had become an acrimonious relationship. No sooner had the couple sat down than they were confronted by two men, who beat them, tied them up, and bundled them into the back of a pickup truck. After a short journey, the pickup stopped.

As the men pulled Ivor out, he could see the lights of Gloucester in front of him, and he realized they were near a steep cliff. It was difficult to see in the dark, but he could make out one of the men picking up the car jack and coming towards him.

'Suddenly I felt a hell of a thud on the back of the head ... I decided to play dead and pretend I was unconscious, but I was fully aware of what was going on.'

The men also attempted and failed to knock Pauline unconscious.

It seems the assassins' idea was to make the attempted

murder look like a driving accident. They put Pauline, who was learning to drive, into the driver's seat of the car. Crucially, the men forgot to move the driver's seat forward. Ivor is six foot one and his wife is five foot two, and these precious inches of difference enabled the Stokles to survive.

The car was set on fire, and the couple then felt the thud of the pickup ramming into the back of it to start it rolling down the thirty-yard slope to the two-hundred-foot drop.

The police estimated that what happened next took Ivor about ten seconds to achieve.

The pain was masked by adrenalin, and Ivor thought, 'Christ! We've got to get out of this car. I swivelled round in the seat, put my shoulders into the door pillar, and kicked Pauline's door open.'

Unaware that Pauline had managed to throw herself out of the car, Ivor struggled in the heat and flames with his own door, his face being severely burned in the process.

'The car was doing about 20 m.p.h. as I rolled out of it and watched it disappear over the cliff, thinking Pauline was still in there,' Ivor remembers.

Both Pauline and Ivor needed extensive and painful plastic surgery, with regular visits to Bristol's Frenchay Hospital. Ivor's injuries were so bad that he was given only a 10 per cent chance of survival. Much of their energy has been channelled into helping each other recover – a process that, however daunting and painful, has nonetheless brought the two of them closer together.

'Any chink in the armour,' says Ivor, 'and we wouldn't be here now.'

Recovery is still a full-time occupation for them both; neither will work again. Ivor's love of horses and harness racing have helped him enormously, and he and Pauline are fully occupied building their own house in a new village.

Ivor has an amazingly philosophical attitude towards their

attackers. 'I get on with life and just enjoy myself. Pauline's a little more bitter about it . . .'

Sheila and her accomplices are still in prison, and Ivor greets the the prospect of their release with equanimity. 'The two blokes have got nothing to gain, and if Sheila tried something the police would know exactly where to find her.'

Things will never be the same again: the physical and mental scars remain. But in some respects life is better.

'Like the smell of grass . . .' Pauline says.

And Ivor agrees: 'It's beautiful – but I never noticed it before. I'm a better person now than I ever was. The people we've met since – I've got my confidence back in the compassion of the human race.'

Carole Gardner also had to face down death, although in very different circumstances from Pauline and Ivor.

In 1988, fourteen-year-old Carole was on a school trip on the cruise ship Jupiter *when it collided with the car-carrier* Adige. *Carole survived, along with all but four of the six-hundred passengers. But the ordeal was not over as she returned home to deal with the emotional aftermath . . .*

A Near-Death Experience
Carole Gardner, 1999

Carole was first aware that something was badly wrong when she heard a very loud bang. The cruise ship, *Jupiter*, on which she was travelling with nearly four hundred other British schoolchildren, had collided with a car-carrier, the *Adige*, in Piraeus harbour.

'The glasses on the bar started sliding down and smashing,' Carole remembers. 'The waiter was trying to catch them. I had this sensation of being tipped to the right.'

Carole didn't realize what had happened until she walked through the dining room. 'There was a big black thing sticking into the side of the ship – the walls all peeled back like a sardine can – and water spraying . . .'

The ship began to list heavily. The lights went out and, in total darkness, Carole fell, smashing her head against some chairs.

'I was disorientated and confused – and then had this feeling of a massive weight slamming me in the back and being pushed really hard up against the chairs. And then another weight and another weight, coming down and down and down . . .' As the ship began to sink, the people behind Carole were sliding down on top of her.

Carole was trapped, but eventually she and some others managed to get out of a nearby door on to the deck, and from there they dived into the sea. The ship was literally sinking beneath them.

'The water was full of grease – I came out covered in black oil. I was treading water as the *Jupiter* sank.'

Carole's mother, Sheila, first heard the news when her mother-in-law called to say she'd heard about a ship sinking in Piraeus harbour on the seven o'clock news. In a state of total disbelief, Carole's parents followed every news broadcast they could tune into. Finally, at one o'clock in the morning, they managed to speak to their daughter on a ship-to-shore phone.

When the children eventually returned home, they had an emotional reunion with their parents in the local church hall. 'I was looking desperately to find my family,' Carole remembers. 'The first face I saw was Dad's poking up from this mass of people – he just gave me the biggest hug I ever had.'

However, the reunion was also the beginning of an emotional backlash, with Carole's feelings rising and falling to alarming degrees. On the first night, Sheila remembers her daughter just wanting to escape into her bedroom. 'She just didn't want to know anybody or anything.'

Later, Carole began to feel elated. 'The world was the most bright and beautiful thing I'd ever seen,' she says – 'like being reborn almost.'

But other feelings surfaced too. Carole felt confused about the emotional turmoil she was experiencing, and she felt guilt at having survived. She even contemplated suicide.

Carole's trauma inevitably had wider implications for her family. Her need for her parents' support caused her sister, Sandra, to feel that she was the 'forgotten one'. Sandra was also confused about the effect of Carole's experience: 'She went away a normal young lady and came back a middle-aged woman, who didn't want to play with Sindy with me or go to the park. I lost my sister to this new person.'

Sandra still feels that she doesn't fully understand what her sister has been through. When the subject of Carole's escape comes up, Sandra is honest enough to admit, 'I don't want to listen sometimes. I have the feeling "Can't we just leave it alone?"'

The sisters' relationship did improve, however, when Carole went to university. 'I'd got my parents to myself for a bit,' Sandra says candidly.

Carole still has good and bad days. The anger and emotion associated with the experience remain, and Sandra and Sheila also still have feelings of vulnerability and pain because of that night.

'As soon as something's wrong, it's wrong and it's never going to be better,' Carole says, describing the black dog that preys on the three of them. In spite of the temptation to give into it, the women remain resilient and determined to forge on – just as Carole did when she clambered out of the ship, despite the weight of people and water pressing against her.

When he was twelve years old, Ken was sexually abused by a family friend. This was the start of an abusive relationship that was to last for several years – a relationship that in fact ended only with the death of the abuser, when Ken was eighteen.

This death precipitated within Ken a range of conflicting emotions and understandable confusion. He's now twenty-six, and is only just coming to terms with his experience.

Ken
2004

Ken met his abuser through football, a sport he played regularly and keenly. He'd known the man, whom his family had come to like and trust, for twelve months before the abuse started.

The man ran a youth club, and every year he took the children to Guernsey for a holiday. Ken's family saw the whole thing as innocent, but when Ken was alone in a car with the man that's where the abuse began. In total, Ken went to Guernsey some fourteen times.

'I didn't tell anyone till later on in life,' Ken says – he kept quiet about the abuse all through his childhood. 'My mum knew that he was single and, the age that he was, she kept warning me just in case anything did happen, I don't think she knew anything, though.'

Ken's feelings about the man were conflicted. To a vulnerable child, the man represented a shoulder to cry on, and Ken remembers the man helping him with a number of problems. But there was always a price to be paid for that help. Moreover – and this seems hard to understand from here – Ken worried that if the truth came out it would destroy the man's standing in the community. And this relationship continued until the man's death, when Ken was eighteen.

'Well, I was there for him,' Ken explains, 'and packed in my job and got him put into hospital and that. And actually he passed away in front of my face in the hospital.'

As he's admitted, Ken's feelings towards the man were confused in a way it's hard to imagine from the outside.

'I wasn't in love with him – it's just that I've never felt that way towards anyone. He made me feel wanted and made me feel as if I had a reason to live. It wasn't because I loved him or nothing, but he did help me out a lot in life.'

After the man died, Ken – rather than feeling liberated – found it hard to cope. Still, the man did reach out to Ken after his death, when he left him money and his house in his will. But that hardly helped Ken either. He started drinking, and turned to crime; there was no one to act as a control in his life.

'I blew it,' Ken says. 'Well, my mum and dad got divorced shortly afterwards. I helped my dad out with £20,000, which was to pay off his half of the divorce towards my mum, which is how much my dad's house was worth at the time. So I paid my mum off. The rest of it I just went out nightclubbing three nights a week.'

The clubbing led to Ken being drunk and disorderly, and then he started stealing from local shops and vehicles. At the time he was doing this Ken had money – from the man's will – and now, with hindsight, he thinks that the crimes were a cry for help. His mum and dad were divorcing and the man had died, all in a short period of time.

'I've come to realize that it was probably a way for me to actually get some help and actually let someone know that I'd got some problems that needed discussing.'

Eventually Ken visited a doctor, who put him on antidepressants. But Ken ended up deliberately overdosing on them. And the crimes continued until he was finally arrested and put on probation, and then his life began to turn itself around. 'Because of seeing someone at the local probation office, they actually were able to help me out.'

One of the areas they obviously tackled, as sensitive as it is, was the question of Ken's sexuality, and whether or not he felt conflicted as a result of his experiences with the abuser. Ken, however, feels no conflict – although the abuse has clearly left a legacy.

'I know exactly where I lie with my sexuality,' he asserts. 'I'm like a normal bloke – after a woman type of thing. It's just I have had problems when it comes to relationships. I ain't the best-looking bloke. Just problems in actually getting a girl-friend at the moment.'

Ken doesn't frequent the pubs, bars and clubs of his past, where he might meet girls, because he's afraid he'll just get back into trouble. Instead, he's channelling his energy into exercise and creating some positive goals to achieve.

'Yes, been doing a lot of working out now, and I've done the London Marathon as well, so I've been training for that. Well, I got a letter come through from the gym saying that there was a charity that they know of that has still got places for the marathon. I applied for the place and got one, and my dad ended up staying with me in London at the hotel, so we sorted out where he was going to meet me and I ran it.'

It's hard to imagine how wonderful that moment must have felt when Ken reached the finishing line with his father waiting for him.

'I'm the only one in the family that's actually done it, so he was really proud of me.'

Ken has now told more of his family about the abuse he suffered, although the response he got might surprise some.

'Well, I've told my youngest brother, and he didn't believe me. He called me sick, because he thought I was making it up. But he's only eighteen or nineteen at the moment, so he wouldn't really understand. And I've also told my mother as well, but she went ballistic because she thought she should have been told sooner.'

Ken's mum was angry with the man, and with Ken for not telling her – particularly as she'd always told him he could come to her if anything was going on, which – obviously finding it very difficult – he never did.

Despite having finally told his family about his experiences, they remain vivid and very much alive for Ken.

'At night, when I'm going to sleep, sometimes I can still see it going over in my head – not the things that was going on, but actually the day he died type of thing. That's the main thing that's actually made it worse for me in my life, because of actually seeing it happening in front of my face.'

And time hasn't helped him to see his experiences in re-assuring black and white. Whatever the abuser did to Ken, he's still able to see the positive impact the man had on his life, and at times he actively misses him – which is an uncomfortable realization for those of us reading Ken's story.

'Obviously I feel as if I wouldn't have even been in trouble with the police if he was still around, because he would have helped me out – that I wouldn't have turned to crime if he was still here.'

Ultimately, however, it's Ken's life and not ours, and how he manages and moves forward is the only important thing. And right now he's feeling very positive.

We'll leave the last word to him: 'I'm very optimistic about the future. But you never know what's around the corner, do you?'

The Giddings family – Tony, Mandy and their children, Laura and Jacob – were on holiday in South Africa at the invitation of Tony's parents. One evening the whole family set off to have a treat – a meal in a Cape Town restaurant. But they never got further than the front door.

Blast Survivors
Tony and Mandy Giddings, 1999

'As we were walking across the room the bomb exploded. At that point the world fell in,' Tony explains. 'It appeared that we'd all been blown in different directions. I found and spoke to both my parents and Mandy, but I never actually found the children immediately after the bomb blast.'

Tony was taken to hospital – but to a different one from his family.

'During that time I had no idea whether they were alive or dead. The emotion was totally indescribable.'

'Luckily the rest of us managed to get into the one ambulance and were all taken to the same hospital,' says Mandy, taking up the story. 'It was chaos. I wanted to be with my children, but they wouldn't allow me to be because I'd had a head injury which they wanted to get sewn up and I was leaving puddles of blood all over their floor.'

Tony's mother, who was the only member of the family not to be injured, went from hospital to hospital in search of Tony.

'It was very easy for me lying there on a hospital trolley saying we need to find Tony,' Mandy continues. 'But she was in Cape Town, she'd lost her glasses, she'd no money, the cellular phone had been blown up, she didn't know where she was, and it was obviously a very difficult thing for her to do. And although she said later that they'd destroyed our family, because we were there at their invitation, I really don't know what I'd have done without her, because I couldn't be with the children but she was and at least they had somebody familiar.'

Three people were killed and twenty-seven injured in the explosion. Mandy and Tony's daughter, Laura, had suffered a serious leg injury which meant amputation.

'She took it very well. I really don't think it hit her for a number of days. She asked me whether it was ever going to come back again, and I said no but we'd get her the best pretend one we possibly could,' Mandy remembers. 'She was terribly depressed, and the only person she would respond to was her little brother. She would just look through you as though you weren't there – which is a heart-rending thing for a parent to see.'

The Giddings made a conscious decision, from day one, to talk about their experiences with their children, so they knew how they felt – that they were scared too, and that such feelings were all right.

'I think that one thing most people don't appreciate is that our "normal" has changed,' Tony explains. 'It's become part of our everyday life that Laura is an amputee and to an extent disabled, and Jacob is a constant worry because he still has shrapnel in his spinal canal and we are very aware that a knock could result in the shrapnel going into his spinal cord and in the worst case could cause paralysis.'

'Jacob is still coming to terms with it,' Mandy continues. 'The other morning he came into the bedroom with his teddy bear wrapped in a blanket and said that Teddy had been blown up and had lost his leg like Laura. It's very difficult to explain to a child that young what happened. Laura has a very good understanding of what happened to her, but in no way feels sorry for herself. She understands that other people died.'

The extraordinary composition shown by Laura seems to be a family trait. The Giddings saw a trauma counsellor – a man who had counselled victims of the Clapham train crash – and after four sessions he sent them away, telling them they were the most together family he had ever encountered.

'The truth is that anyone who finds themselves in the circumstances that we did, or similar circumstances, well you have two choices: either you get on with it or it takes you down, and you go under,' Tony says, explaining the family philosophy. 'I hope to spend more time with my children and actually enjoy them. Perhaps like most fathers I was so busy with bringing an income into the family that I tended to overlook the children, and I'm not going to let that happen again.'

'We just get on with life, because it puts life into perspective,' Mandy adds. 'You really don't know what's going to happen in the next five minutes, and so we live every day as though it's possibly our last.'

Questions were on Jo Bunting's mind, at the beginning and at the end of a nightmare evening. Admittedly, 'Which city had the first pavements?' hardly cuts to the core of one's being as dilemmas go. But on that fine night when Jo bounced across her local to greet her friends and down the first refreshing gin and tonic, she little expected the horrifying humiliation that was to ensue . . .

Pub Quiz
Jo Bunting, 2004

'I made my way across the crowded room towards my two friends and soon to be teammates,' Jo explained, naive optimism still present in her voice. 'I was about to embark on an anecdote about a temperamental parking meter I'd just experienced, when I became aware that they looked slightly flustered and ill at ease and were fixing me with accusing eyes.'

'You're late – it's already started,' hissed one.

'Oh, right,' Jo replied, outwardly cheerful but inwardly suddenly feeling a very slight sense of doom. 'Well, not to worry,' she thought – 'I'll get the drinks in.'

'Forget the drinks. Which city had the first pavements?'

Jo blinked: 'This is going to be a nightmare, isn't it?'

Fast-forward two and half hours and Jo was leaving the pub, her first quiz behind her. Confidence shattered and clutching a large bag of pasta – a curiously metaphorical wooden spoon – she cut a humiliated and exhausted figure.

In the third round the three amigos were informed by the energetic quizmaster – who Jo suspected didn't otherwise get out much – that all the answers would begin with the letter S.

'We leaned forward with relief,' Jo explained. Well, at least that gave them a clue. 'Our shaky confidence was shattered by a loud roar, courtesy of the quizmaster,' she continued.

'What S is an apothecary's weight of 20 grains?'

The three friends looked at each other. In what was to become a familiar scenario, they realized that not only did they not know the answer, they didn't actually under stand the question.

'Literature now,' shouted our host, to cheers from the room. 'Which S wrote . . .'

'Do you know, I think I'm going to have to make a move,' one third of Jo's team said.

'You said this would be fun,' she almost spat the words out. 'It's like doing an exam with a bag of pork scratchings thrown in.'

And then they were two. 'My remaining teammate and I struggled on as gamely as we could, and in a strange kind of way we bonded – perhaps because we were equally determined to see it through to the bitter end; perhaps because we were relieved to find that we were both equally thick. Either way, I can pinpoint with some precision the moment we hit rock bottom.'

At the end of each round they had to pass their answers to

the team at the neighbouring table, to be marked.

'I haven't heard such muffled hilarity before or since,' Jo said quietly. 'The question-master plodded through the answers until he reached this one: "Which word has entered 1,200 different languages but remains the same both in spelling and pronunciation in each of them?"'

The answer is of course 'Amen'. Cue cheers from around the room.

'Remind me what we put,' Jo muttered across the table.

But her friend was avoiding her eyes.

'The answer was "Amen",' Jo repeated. 'What did we put?'

Her friend looked up and quietly administered the killer blow. 'Burger,' she said.

2

Itchy Feet

Travel always provided a rich and varied source of inspiration for the contributors to Home Truths. *The hapless coach party of thirty-four academics, for instance, which mysteriously turned into thirty-three without anyone remembering who had gone missing and with the thirty-fourth scholar never reappearing. Drivers wearing hats and Volvos with their ever-shining headlights were other subjects that exercised listeners over the years. And can anyone forget the sighting of a pig, riding pillion? Almost an urban myth in the making.*

Still, as we're about to discover, even the shortest journey can demand Sisyphus-like stoicism. You don't need to be trekking to the South Pole with only a couple of dachshunds for company. You could just be going to school.

Maurice O'Connell is a university lecturer and also runs a recycling centre in Cornwall, an interest he might have developed as a child witnessing his parents' efforts at recycling their car, and in fact recycling bits of furniture and their farm to incorporate into their car. That, however, was the least of Maurice's problems. Like a lot of good O'Connells, Maurice came from Dublin – well, fifteen miles from Dublin. Near enough you might say, but then you didn't have to go to school with Maurice's four siblings. The school bus was OK. It was the car that was the problem . . .

School Run
Maurice O'Connell, 2005

'We'd all climb into the car, which – and this is the important point – was a Fiat 600,' Maurice explained.

Now, a Fiat 600 is not a capacious vehicle. In fact, as Maurice puts it, 'It's a bit like a Mini, but smaller.'

Or a tin can on wheels.

'I'm now in my late thirties, and I'm approximately six foot four,' Maurice said. 'Which is the average height in my family. My dad is six foot three-ish, and was approximately eighteen stone.'

The picture that's emerging is a bit like one of those 'how many students can you get in a Mini?' *Guinness Book of Records* photos. In other words, impossible.

'No, it doesn't sound possible at all. Basically, with a lot of flexibility and squashing, and the school bags and other sports items all sort of stacked on top of us, you just pushed, basically – one person behind the driver, and the rest would gradually sort of wriggle and shove, and elbows would be intertwined and arms interlocked.'

You begin to wonder, with all those interlocking limbs, how they managed to close the doors. Was Mrs O'Connell outside like a Tokyo train employee, squeezing the doors shut?

'No, no, everything was fine. We all managed to squash in tightly. There wasn't any sort of major squeezing or bending of the car. I mean,' Maurice continued, slightly surprised at the recollection, 'this was the quite strange thing – the car seemed perfectly fine about it all.'

The car was probably muttering under its breath . . .

Still, the strapping O'Connells were now firmly ensconced in their Fiat. So how was the journey?

'The car didn't have a radio, but we were all very keen on listening to the news in the morning, so a portable radio would be brought with us and that would be in the front seat with the passenger, and their job would be to tune the radio in and keep the volume high enough. The windows would be quite steamy, given that there were six people in the car,' Maurice remembers, not altogether fondly, 'and there wasn't very good ventilation in these Fiats. There was a little lever under the back passenger seat, which opened up to let warm air in from the engine. That was the ventilation,' he added ruefully.

Despite the unrelenting discomfort meted out on a daily basis, the brothers seemed pretty accepting of their fate.

'We would lose the control of our limbs and the power of our legs after about fifteen or twenty minutes,' Maurice said quite matter of factly. 'And then the shoving and elbowing and sort of shifting of buttocks on the seat would begin. But we were quite co-operative with each other, because we'd have to do it the next day, again.'

It's at this point that one begins to wonder what other people made of this daily spectacle – a family of strapping giants squashed into the smallest car on the roads. Maybe they got used to it.

'Well,' Maurice admitted, 'there were always the very concerned fellow travellers looking at our faces squashed against the window, and the steam, and all the bits and pieces piled up. And there were sort of polite smiles as we were going by.'

You might imagine that the O'Connells' journey was troublesome enough without the need to insert further complications. But you'd be wrong . . .

As Maurice explained, 'We needed to get the newspapers while we were on the journey, so one of the tasks for the person in the front seat – when the car slowed down in the traffic – was to jump out and run to the nearest newsagent, grab the *Irish Times*, and then wait for us in the car to trundle past in the slow traffic, or catch up with the car if the traffic had cleared. And because it was sort of rush hour and a busy time, it could be quite a distance before you managed to find space to slow down again.'

So, if you thought beating one of your four strapping brothers to the front seat would have been like winning the pools, think again.

'You were sent out', Maurice added – just to really bring the point home – 'not knowing when you'd get back into the car, or if you'd get back for maybe two or three miles.'

Maybe they should have caught the bus. But family camaraderie was clearly a stronger bond than common sense. So, now an out-of-breath O'Connell has clambered back into the car with the papers, which with luck weren't the two tons of forest they are today. After all, if a Fiat 600 is a tiny car, the chances are it has a tiny engine.

'There was a hill, just in the last two miles of the journey.'

You sort of knew there would be.

'Which was a slow rising slope over half a mile – a bit more – and there's no way that the car could make it up the hill with all of us. So it was decided to offload the ballast – which was us.'

Not the *Irish Times* or the radio . . .

'We would leave our school bags in the back of the car and then climb out. We'd straighten our legs and arms, and then we'd walk up the hill while my dad drove all the way up to the top. Then he would basically read the newspaper and wait for us to catch up. And again, because we were all in different states of fitness as well, we wouldn't always arrive at the same time.'

Regardless of the grief and strain the O'Connells inflicted on it, the car remained a reliable and loyal servant. Despite Maurice's father breaking the driver's seat and pulling the accelerator pedal off. His father wasn't the most practical of men, and didn't seem to realise that his size might have some part to play in the bits falling off the poor little Fiat.

Fortunately, Mrs O'Connell was a bit more practical – mending the driver's seat by propping it up with an old table leg.

'Her role in the vehicles was to start them, fix them and mend them, whereas my father broke them, bent them and got stuck in places with them,' Maurice said, explaining how his parents shared out their responsibilities.

That, you will have noticed, was a bit of a detour from the odyssey of the school run. So, we've reached the summit of the hill, and from here it's pretty plain sailing until the O'Connells reach the school.

'My dad managed to get out with a huge amount of dignity. But the rest of us could take ten minutes, because the legs would have gone to sleep by then. Usually the front passenger would pull up the seat and extract all the bags and stuff like that, and gradually pull us all slowly out. But because our legs were asleep we had to hang on to the car while the circulation came back, and then we'd straighten ourselves out and march in, in the proper manner, into the school.'

Knowing what children are like, it doesn't take much to imagine that this ritual could turn into a piece of uproarious daily theatre. And boys being boys . . .

'On one or two occasions,' Maurice remembered, 'the car was lifted up and hidden behind a hedge.'

Not a very respectful way to treat a car that behaved so unstintingly and with such quiet dignity.

Of course, the Fiat has long gone to that big car lot in the sky. And as an epilogue to this tale of contrary behaviour Maurice explained what his father is driving now there's just him and Mrs O'Connell, and no six foot four inch sons to transport around.

'Now they drive quite spacious vehicles,' Maurice said, puzzlement bubbling away as he spoke. 'They don't carry anybody in them, they drive by themselves.'

School days, eh? The best days of your life.

Tom Bussman, who has obviously never met Maurice O'Connell's father, considers that 'vainglory', one of the Seven Deadly Sins, is best observed among car-lovers . . .

Car Appeal

Tom Bussman, 1998

Vainglory goes beyond mere blind self-approval and into the rarified realm of flaunting. It calls for a degree of dedication to one's own self-image normally confined to politicians or the acting profession.

'Am I above all this?' Tom asks, redundantly. 'Far from it. I was once the possessor of a ludicrously overpowered and over-priced four-wheel penile substitute: a Porsche Carrera convertible.'

Tom's long-suffering family, to their credit, by and large refused to be seen in the thing.

'If I ever offered to do the school run, my sensitive children demanded to be set down a good half-mile from the school gates. Should they be seen by any fellow pupils, the line was that a plausible kidnapper had enticed them into the vehicle, and only quick wits plus basic karate had ensured their escape. Even at the zenith, or nadir, of Thatcherism – depending on your politics – a bus pass carried far more street cred than a ride in Daddy's Porsche.'

All too rarely, vainglory brings with it comeuppance.

'I was ready to take a kid or two on the Saturday pilgrimage, top-down, engine throbbing, to "Toys 'R' Them". Only problem, I can't find my **** wallet. There then ensues my usual frenzy – ignored, as usual, by my family. My other half, teeth welded through habit, leaves me to it and sets out on foot with offspring as I contemplate whole-sale telephonic credit-card massacre. Not in the best of tempers, I wrench open the door of my status symbol and wrestle down the hood. I then click on my seatbelt and, would you believe it, next to my seat is my wallet. What a happy chap I am!

'I join the traffic and start off up the road at 4.9 m.p.h., my lips going brrrrm, brrrrm. Joys of spring? Definitely. There, ahead, is my grim-spined spouse with handfuls of sprogs heading for the horrors of the Northern Line. My chance to cheer her up, wouldn't you say? As I draw level, I wave my newly found wallet, tooting my horn the while. At which point comes my comeuppance – big time. I suddenly see myself as others must see me: a balding man in a Porsche Carrera convertible, waving his wallet to passers-by. The horror! It was as though I had become the central character in a Franz Kafka nightmare, and woken up to find myself converted into – Michael Winner. Aargh!'

Travel tales are frequently filled with hardships and privations. Mostly these involve being four thousand miles away from the nearest human in broiling temperatures with just a couple of shifty-looking lizards to eat and a cactus leaf to drink from. Or hanging from a glacial mountain by a piece of string.

It might be cruel, if accurate, to suggest that alcohol played a role in Helen Wingate Marsh's tale, both in her predicament and in her response to it. But, as you will see, when the water got choppy Helen retained a millpond-like sense of calm.

Stowaway
Helen Wingate Marsh, 2002

Back in 1974, shortly before Christmas, Helen, a former merchant seawoman, was working as a postwoman in

Southampton. One afternoon she nipped off to meet up with her former crewmates on board her last ship, the SS *Oranje*. To cut a long story short, it was a marathon session, involving a lot of alcohol and a drunken return to 'Lady Helen's', as she was known to her friends. The next morning, with time short before the *Oranje* set off on her next voyage to South Africa, Helen and her pals, bleary-eyed, set off for the docks, making it back to the ship with just enough time to spare for yet another farewell drink on board – or the hair of the dog as it's known in medical circles.

'As I was downing my fifth Bacardi and Coke,' explains Helen, 'I looked out of the porthole and thought, "Oh! God almighty!"'

What she had seen was The Needles which meant the ship was on its way to South Africa – with Helen on board.

Hauled up in front of the chief officer, Helen was designated a stowaway and promptly locked in the hospital – keel-hauling, presumably, being too good for her, and making her walk the plank likely to upset the paying customers. The very modern plan was to set her down at the ship's first stop, at Las Palmas.

Meanwhile, back home, Helen's mother, who'd been looking after her six-year-old grandson for the day, received a phone call on Helen's behalf, informing her that her daughter was on board a ship steaming for South Africa, and was she willing to pay the round fare? She wasn't. Nor was she overly amused by her daughter's unscheduled absence.

Back on board, Helen was clad only in her Post Office coat and was carrying nothing but a comb – a curious choice for the sole possession to carry on your person even around Southampton's terra firma, you might think, let alone at sea. So she had to make do with a whip-round from the crew and her friends, until she was put down in Las Palmas. There she was befriended by an English family, who invited her for

Christmas lunch. So, instead of catching the first available flight home to confront an irate mother, she donned her paper hat and tucked into a yuletide feast, Canary Islands style.

It was a full two weeks later when Helen finally made it back to familiar shores on the good ship *Edinburgh Castle*.

'I was a DBS, which is either a Distressed or a Displaced British Subject,' Helen explained. 'I wasn't at all distressed – just a little apprehensive about being reunited with my mother!'

Her immediate reception committee consisted of Customs and Excise, Immigration and Special Branch, all of whom wanted to have a word with her.

Oddly enough, Helen's employers, the Post Office, were probably the most understanding. 'The supervisor knew I'd gone for a drink on board, and said, "I bet that silly mare's on her way to South Africa!"'

And she was.

Janet Graves proposed an extraordinary theory of navigation. Give it go – and let us know where you end up . . .

Navigation Theory

Janet Graves, 2001

'I wonder if you might be interested in how I find my way to where I want to go without using a map?' Janet asks, rhetorically. 'I've been using the probability theory for over twenty years. It's probably why my ten-year-old daughter gave me a book of road maps for Christmas, and why she often says, "Are we lost, mummy?" To which I reply, "No, dear, we're just not there yet."'

Janet's 'probability theory' involves following someone who is *probably* going her way.

'Today, coming from Liverpool to Manchester, I followed a single man in a suit in what might have been a company car and who was probably going to Manchester. He was. In twenty odd years I have only once followed a driver up their own drive to their garage.'

Janet, it appears, isn't the only one to take this approach.

'I thought I was alone in using the probability theory, till my friend Tricia told me how she found her way to the new John Lewis store which had opened near Manchester. She simply followed a woman in a car who looked like she was probably going shopping there. In the event, she was going shopping – but at the Trafford Centre near Manchester, where Tricia spent a happy day instead.'

Every cloud has a silver lining.

In fact, as it turns out, Janet Graves is very much not alone with her route-management theory. Drivers are doing it everywhere. Even in Germany . . .

Follow that Car!
Kevin Elam, 2001

'My girlfriend quickly found her target – a green Opel Kadet,' Kevin remembers, ruefully. 'It cut through the Cologne traffic with an assurance and confidence that shamed us. So we followed. After about half an hour the green Kadet pulled over and two of the car's three occupants casually got out and entered a shop. We dutifully pulled over and waited too. The two men were in the shop some time, and I remember thinking, "What on earth are they buying in there?" About twenty minutes later the two men emerged from the shop and walked casually back to the car. The green Opel then pulled away and we followed.'

Initially Kevin thought their luck was in, as the Opel headed out of town on the roads they'd failed to find. But his confidence was soon shattered when he looked in the mirror and saw an army of blue flashing lights.

'One of the police cars drew level with us, and a gun-brandishing officer waved us over. Slowly, anxiously, I pulled our car over to the side of the road. But the police didn't slow down or stop. Instead, the posse picked up speed and sped on. In the distance we could see the green Opel flooring it too!

'The moral of this tale is clear,' Kevin adds. 'Never, ever, follow a strange car. You never know what you'll end up in!'

Are you paying attention Janet?

Linda Gilbert's grandmother was a great traveller and walker. When she was struck with osteoarthritis, that seemed an end to her hikes. But Vera was a redoubtable woman...

Vera's Voyages
Linda Gilbert, 2002

One of Vera's passions was hillwalking with her husband, Sidney. Often she would sit in front of a map with a pin, close her eyes, and stick the pin in the map – then she would go to Thomas Cook and book a flight to as near as she could get to that place.

When she developed osteoarthritis in both hips Vera really resented her loss of freedom. What's more, she'd never learned to drive. Then she heard about a government scheme which supplied three-wheeled 'trikes' to disabled people. Vera applied for one, and learned to drive it. She was granted her first car (small, pale blue, with only one seat) during the 1960s. Occasionally Linda would cram in for an illicit ride.

'Most people', Linda remembers, 'used their three-wheeled car to go shopping and visit nearby family and friends, but not Vera. She headed out on the highways and byways of the countryside – Yorkshire, Scotland and the Lake District – single-handedly negotiating the motorways of Great Britain. Other motorists used to think it was illegal for her car to ride the motorways, but it wasn't – her car's engine qualified her to do so.'

The only downside was the single seat, which meant that poor old Sidney had to travel separately, by train or bus, and arrange to meet up when they both arrived at their destination. In the end, Vera's disability grew worse, which prevented her from driving at all. But for the time she had that little blue trike she had been granted several precious extra years of liberty.

Sometimes it's not the getting there but the journey itself that captures the imagination of Home Truths *listeners. Or, to be more precise, it's specific sections of roads and motorways that send them into transports of delight . . .*

My Favourite Road
Sue Elliott-Nichols, 2001

Sue and her husband Tony's favourite road is the A470. That little collection of letters and numbers hides a wealth of scenery.

'It is the most beautiful road,' raves Sue. 'It leads from Cardiff to Betws-y-coed in Snowdonia. The first time we went there was when we were first in love!'

Tony reels off a number of towns, villages and beauty spots along the route, and Sue waxes lyrical. 'As you enter Snowdonia National Park it's so exciting – the rolling landscape suddenly becomes so bleak!'

As Sue and Tony drive through one of the forests on the A470, the ice and snow thickly covering the trees bring the lyrical Welshman out in Tony. 'It's very magical, very Snow-Fairyish!'

Very.

The Ewell Bypass – or, to be exact, the busy section leading to Kingston via Tolworth – brings an emotive response from listener Margaret Atwood (no, not that one).

'I was brought up in the country, where roads were soft grey things that wound through green hedges and fields and trees. When I first came to London, I just couldn't believe this road. It was wide, full of cars, with the houses right by the road. And then there were messages all over it, telling you what to do – stop here; turn right – and traffic lights, and things to read on long poles! I worked in this area for thirty years, and each time I drove along this road I felt a longing to be back in the country. Then I felt a strange sort of guilt – people lived here, and I felt my hatred was doing them a disservice. From the guilt grew the feeling that if I'm ever punished this is where I'll have to live. Now I live in Dorset again, I feel a strange sort of pleasure: I only go along it for nice reasons – to visit friends.'

For Robin Smith, it's the M25 which is a bit of a turn-on.

'I don't know if I'm sad or just appreciating the workmanship that goes into building the infrastructure.'

Approaching junction 21A – the turn off for the M1 – brings poetic language to Robin's lips. 'I get a feeling of calm as I go over it and look down, seeing the traffic from four different ways, all underneath and around you. There's about twenty-four lanes,' says Robin. 'Someone has worked out the traffic forecast, drawn it, built it, and we just use it and ignore it! You can feel passionate about anything – even roads.'

Asked if he likes Spaghetti Junction, Robin is dismissive: 'I think that's really overrated!'

As a schoolboy, Quentin Howard was a sort of timetable prodigy. Whether, as with so many before him, his talent dwindled with age he was reticent about confirming, but as a nine-year-old he was a veritable Einstein.

His four older brothers – fools that they were – simply caught the number 63, a mere two hundred yards from their front door, right to the school gates. Quentin took an entirely different journey to the same destination, which – he maintains to this day – gave him an important advantage over his siblings.

Getting to School
Quentin Howard, 2005

'If I timed it right,' Quentin explained, 'I could not only leave later than them but I could arrive at a reasonable time and not get a detention. So my routine was to leave the house at ten past eight and walk half a mile down the road past the sweet shop – very tempting – to go to the railway station in Ben Rhydding.'

There, Quentin would catch the 08.23 and travel the ten miles to Shipley, arriving at 08.46. Assuming, of course, that he didn't succumb to the lure of that sweet shop and miss his train. As if he'd do that.

Shipley town centre, where the corporation buses stopped, was five hundred yards from the station. But Quentin didn't walk to the bus terminus, oh no . . .

'If I caught a red bus, I could catch that half a mile up the hill and then change to a corporation bus. The reason I did it was that you could save a halfpenny by doing that. And the corporation bus would deliver me to school within three hundred yards. I'd walk the rest of the way and sail in through the gates half a minute before they closed and you got a detention.'

If Quentin's connections all connected he'd arrive at school at nine-oh-four-and-a-half. It seems he was fortunate to go to the only school in Britain that closed its gates at five past nine. Well, not exactly, as he went on to explain. The school day started at nine on the dot. But a pupil who came from a long way away, or had a difficult journey, could apply for a five minute extension.

'So,' Quentin continued, 'I applied for that. Got my five-minute extension, and that allowed me to use the train and the buses and the walking.'

And why did Quentin do this, when, let's not forget, his brothers just climbed on to a bus outside their house and climbed out of the bus outside the school?

'Because you could. There was a system there that was designed to allow, to accommodate, people like that, so I thought, "Well, I'll do it." But the joy for me was travelling on the train' – Quentin was warming to his subject now – 'because that was a much more sophisticated means of transport than a horrible old corporation bus, you know, with people throwing your satchel about.' And, heaven forbid, your various bus and railway timetables.

Quentin took the same two-bus-one-train journey back home. But again the pesky school day interfered with his plans. What were the education authorities thinking?

'Because of the time of the train, I had to get an early bus and leave school ten minutes early. So I actually shaved fifteen minutes off my school day.'

And all he had to do was walk up the road (past the sweet shop), catch a train, catch a bus, to catch . . . Well you get the idea. Amazingly, perhaps, no one – neither his brothers nor the school – cottoned on.

'You'd think the school would have said, "Hang on, Howard, H. Q., why are you having this early pass and your brothers don't?" But they didn't. So I just used the system that was there to be used.'

Quentin's motivation for such a tortuous journey was a younger brother's desire to be different. He didn't want to just fall in behind the other four on the well-trodden path to the corporation bus stop, but wanted to strike out for individuality – something he has continued throughout his life. What is more, Quentin had travel options. He wasn't just tied to the schedule described so lovingly above.

'There were little deviations you could take,' he reminisced. 'Instead of getting out at Shipley and going up the hill into the town, I could go down to Canal Road and catch a different red bus, which would take me and deliver me at the school playing fields.' The big advantage being – no prefects. So, if Quentin was late, he could sneak in without incurring the school's wrath. After all, it's hard to imagine that Quentin's route didn't go wrong – often.

'But this was the sixties, remember,' Quentin disagrees – 'when transport used to work. I'd love to go back and try the journey now, to see if it was possible. I can remember all the times – 08.23, 08.46, 08.55 . . .'

Somehow, that doesn't come as much of a surprise.

Anyone reading this story involved in industry, manufacturing or logistics – that's jargon for trucks, by the way – will probably recognize Quentin's school journey as an early example of 'just in time' delivery. And he was saving a penny every day – a king's ransom back in the sixties.

'I could buy two half-penny chews, or one of those sherbet flying saucers. That was a real treat. But, if I saved them up long enough, once a year on my birthday – or for some other treat – I could travel on the train in first class instead of second class. And of course that was a great experience, because I would go into the plush, red, velvety seats where all these crusty old men with their *Financial Times* would look over their half-rimmed glasses at me.'

And they'd be looking at a nine-year-old whippersnapper and thinking, 'What is he doing in here? Wait till the conductor catches you.' But that was Quentin's coup de maître.

'When the guard came in, expecting to throw me out, I would proudly produce my ticket, and I had a first-class ride and I felt like a king.'

A king who got up people's noses and felt good at the same time.

Quentin had to agree: 'Well, I suppose so. I wouldn't quite put it like that, but yes I did.'

When you're on the road, in between following any available vehicle because it might know where it's going and admiring the camber and the tarmacadam seal on the highway, you might find it useful to take note of a Pottingerism or two. Never heard of them? Well, here's a clue.

Pottingerisms
Peter Stewart, 2001

'Actually, a Pottingerism is an event first noted and described by my friend Arthur . . . Pottinger,' Peter explains – 'the world-famous Shetland folk/country-and-western singer, now based in Orkney.

'Imagine that you're in your car driving along a road – just an ordinary road, anywhere – minding your own business and paying full attention to the road and the world around you. Lo and behold, you notice there's a car coming the other way, also obviously minding its own business and threatening no one.

'But wait. What's that just about midway between you and the oncoming vehicle? It's a bicycle. And, it's the only other thing in sight, apart from the car coming the other way and now substantially closer. It's the only other thing that's been on the road for the last twenty . . . two hundred miles.

'The other car is getting pretty close, and so is the bicycle, and they are getting very close. It's no use: it's quite obvious that the point of passing the car will also involve passing the bicycle. One will have to slow down and give way. That is a Pottingerism. That is Pottinger's Law. The oncoming vehicle and the bicycle will always conflict, exactly.'

For 'bicycle' you can substitute 'horse', 'telegraph pole', 'pedestrian', 'parked car'. Although they do not strictly create Pottingerisms, the rule still applies. The point is that 'it', whatever 'it' might be, will always, on an otherwise clear road, conflict with whatever vehicle decides to be on the other side of the road coming towards you.

Pottinger's Law. Good old Arthur.

3

Blood is Thicker than Water

❧

Cabbies learning to sing so they can serenade their old dads, sons shirking music practice, fathers becoming mothers – yes, you read that right – and families who never talk: Home Truths *heard from them all, and many more. By turns funny, embarrassing, shocking and moving, their strories vividly prove that old adage 'You can choose your friends, but you can't pick your relatives.'*

Maddie and Tim Aldridge are divorced. They have three sons and a daughter, Tilly, who's fourteen. The custody arrangement is that the young persons spend weekdays at their mother's house and weekends at their father's not all that far away in south London. The upshot of this is that Tilly has two bedrooms. For Tilly, as for most of us, especially those in their teens, bedrooms are important, highly personal places. But in Tilly's case the two rooms, like the two halves of her life, are very different.

Tilly Two Rooms
Tilly Aldridge, 2004

'I spend most of my time up here. I love it in my room. You have to have your own space, otherwise you're not comfortable,' Tilly explains. 'If anything's going wrong in the house, you'll always be safe in your room – you always come up here

61

knowing that no one can follow you. I think every teenage girl now goes through the phase where they just don't want to go out of their room because everything is in here that entertains them.'

Tilly describes her room at her mother's house as 'tasteful, modern and comfortable'. The house itself is a vision of gorgeous, white loveliness. Apart, that is, from the fingermarks on the walls . . .

She keeps her room pretty tidy – for a teenager – admitting that when she's in a bad mood and has nothing better to do she'll tidy it up. 'A teenager in a bad mood?' I hear you say. 'That room must be spotless.'

On the subject of moods, it appears that Tilly and her mother, Maddie, have come to a somewhat unusual entente on how Tilly's room is decorated.

'Well, we never argued about it,' Tilly says. 'She chose most of the things that go in here, but I don't mind it at all. It makes me feel a little bit more grown up. Also, my mum picks out things and says, 'This doesn't work,' and so she says, 'Take it over to Dad's house,' and I go on over there and just dump it there.'

Just dump it there – a novel solution. What Tilly dumps are all the things that clash with Maddie's white walls and tasteful decor. Posters for a start – unless they're on the specially mounted board. 'If Mum saw the paint coming off the wall then she'd go mad.' And Tilly admits that given half a chance she'd splash around some colour too.

The other thing that Maddie can't stand is stuffed animals. They go straight round to Dad's. However, in the corner of the room there's a doll's house. Not your average, common-or-garden doll's house, but a very modern one: from Bauhaus to doll's house, so to speak. 'Yeah, it's quite different,' Tilly says coolly. 'Sort of adds to the effect that I'm still a child. I don't play with it often.

'When I go round to friends' houses their rooms are always really messy,' Tilly continues. 'It's a really nice room. I love it, but I know my friends think it's actually quite a boring bedroom.'

A bedroom that Tilly cleans herself. A very different room to the one at her dad's house, because Dad doesn't care one jot what she puts in it, as long as she's happy.

Maddie, it won't surprise you to learn, hopes with a passion that Tilly will take after her: 'I would be absolutely devastated I think if she did do that sort of chintzy, big-sofas, big-curtain thing.'

You might expect a child to dislike commuting between two parents – the transience of it. But Tilly sees only advantages.

'I think I probably prefer it to having one life at one house, because I reckon that's pretty boring. But I've got two houses I can go to, and there's always going to be a charge in the atmosphere between brothers and me and parents, and in the end it's quite nice.

'Sometimes,' she continues, 'I feel like I've been carted from one place to the other. It's not bad that feeling – it's not as bad as everyone thinks having your parents split up. In the end it's sort of for the best, so it doesn't really bother you in the end.'

Nonetheless, Tilly is moving between different worlds, and she does have to adapt to each. Still, she recognizes that, all things considered, she has it luckier than lots of other children of divorced parents. Her dad has a house, which feels like home, rather than some poky little flat. And her parents have been brilliant at making it easy for her to adapt too.

Tilly had tidied up a bit before *Home Truths* descended on her bedroom at Tim's, but it was still a long way from the pristine, calm space at Maddie's.

'It's a complete mess, and you can't usually see the floor

because there are clothes everywhere, bags everywhere,' she admits.

The walls are a deep blue – they were pink, but Tilly changed her mind so painted them over. She changes her mind quite often. Stuffed animals litter the room, which is a lot more jumbled and higgledy-piggledy than the room at Maddie's.

'Yeah, it's sort of more interesting to look at,' Tilly says.

If only her mother could hear her. There's also a hanging rail raised right up to the ceiling with a winch, which holds all Tilly's dressing-up clothes from when she was younger.

Not only are the rooms very different, but Tilly is conscious of behaving differently in each house.

'I care much more about the other room than this one. My dad doesn't really care what it looks like, and Mum does care what my bedroom looks like at home. He wouldn't even give a toss. He might ask, "Oh, I saw you've got some posters up." And then I say, "yes." And he would just sort of walk out. But that's about it. He only just let me get some pets and keep them in my room.'

The pets are not immediately visible in the chaos of the room. But then they appear, partially obscured behind the clothes and toys: hamsters. It's hard to imagine hamsters living in Maddie's house.

The room with the hamsters and the blue walls is in what was the family house before Tim and Maddie separated, which makes it that bit different and a bit more special for Tilly.

'Dad kept this house and Mum went and bought another one, but I feel much more at home here, as it's sort of where we first lived and everything. And Dad doesn't mind me having a lot of friends round to stay the night, if they're kept in my room. This house has changed a lot since Mum doesn't live here any more. It's actually got so much more messier and not sort of homelike. I like them both a lot.'

'I'm keen that they should identify this house as being home,' Tim explains, 'and therefore be able to personalize their rooms. From my point of view I quite like it also because it reminds me of them when they're not here. I let them get on, and it's her den. I think she uses it a bit too much as bolt-hole from the boys.'

'Well, I like it up here. The boys don't really like coming in here.'

Tilly and her brothers don't get on. 'I don't think there's one time when we've had a civilized conversation for about three years.'

'I think that's excessive,' Tim says. 'Tilly's fourteen, Henry's eleven, Barnaby is seven, and Bruno is four. It's not that bad – you do get on . . .'

'Dad!' she interjects. 'All you do is shout at us for bickering, because we always argue.'

'Well, I'm just conscious of the whole house being a complete tip and not knowing where everything is,' Tim explains.

'You have a cleaner,' Tilly says.

'I do have a cleaner, but she just tidies a bit. My big plan is to get in a firm of contract cleaners.'

'You should go on that programme – *How Clean is Your House?* – with the two women.'

'I don't think I need to air my dirty linen in public in that regard.'

'Well, it's worth a try, because this house is a tip.'

'I don't think it's unhygienic. It's just messy.'

Well, it's certainly messier than Maddie's.

'Yes,' Tim continues, warming to his theme. 'Friends come round to watch football matches on the television, because they can do so here without fear of wives being upset by vast crowds of smoking men, swilling beer, in their drawing room, and I find myself tidying up halfway through the evening.

When I had a chap living here with me, in one of the other rooms, it was known as the *Men Behaving Badly* house. He's now moved out.'

'It was actually known as "all the divorced men living together in one house",' Tilly adds.

Or, to be precise, three single men living together, with all their various children turning up at various times.

'Yes. The New Cross Home for Dysfunctional Fathers. We even had eight children in the house,' Tim says.

'It would be like a children's home,' Tilly adds acerbically.

'That did put strain on things from time to time.'

'It was kind of horrible, madness. It was good fun. Because I was living with my best friend it was good fun. But then occasionally it wasn't, because you did get kind of tired of each other.'

Tilly describes her room at Tim's as outgoing and fun, more jumbled, more colourful and comfortable. But she also craves the peace and calm of her room at Maddie's. You wouldn't expect to think this of a child with divorced parents, but it looks like she's got the best of both worlds.

If you think the dichotomy between Maddie's and Tim's abodes is just bad old stereotyping, then consider how the personalities of Simon and Jane Higgs manifest themselves in their cars. After all, Simon and Jane share a house. Jane's car is sleek, clean and perfumed. Simon's is a dump.

Car Wars
Simon Higgs, 2000

Simon Higgs and his wife, Jane, have a busy job each, and four children between them. They each have a car too.

66

'Daddy's car is very messy,' says Simon's nine-year-old daughter, Bethany, with considerable understatement.

The interior of Simon's car is a veritable Aladdin's cave of cassettes, work papers, tobacco wrappers, crisp packets, and a grand total of twenty-two drinks cans.

'I look upon my car as a bachelor pad,' says Simon. 'I'm forced into tidiness in the house. I enjoy the squalor of the interior, and I play my music loud. I lose years when I'm sitting in the car.'

Closer inspection unearths yet more debris: a Polo mint packet, more cassettes, letters, chocolate-bar covers, a chocolate-bar cover covered in chocolate, empty cigarette packets, and melted chocolate inside a chocolate cover.

'I wonder if it's still edible . . ?' Simon says, unashamed, eyeing the melted chocolate.

'We don't really refuse to go in Daddy's car,' Bethany says. 'But we do prefer to go in Mummy's car.'

Jane's car, soft music playing in the background, couldn't be more different. It looks like it has never left the showroom.

'I have my cloths and things for wiping it,' explains Jane.

The neatness is almost palpable.

'And I've got my air fresheners,' she adds, 'The housework is hard going with the children. This is a smaller area that's easier to keep under control – it's separate from the house. It's my car.'

Parents, it seems, are able to find an infinite number of ways to embarrass their children. We all know the feeling – many of us from both sides. Philippa Budgen endured a childhood of serial embarrassment at the hands of her mother, Madeleine. There was the noisy Cortina, the ever-present smell of lambing. And what Maddie Aldridge would have made of Madeleine's mauve polka dot dress doesn't bear thinking about.

Embarrassing Mum
Philippa Budgen, 2002

Philippa Budgen's mother, Madeleine, has just bought a new lilac outfit, which reminds them both of various embarrassing incidents in the past. Madeleine recalls a sports day when she was wearing what she thought was a perfectly unexceptional mauve dress with white polka dots. Phillipa, however, took violent exception to it, and told her mother that she had humiliated her beyond belief by wearing it.

'You went slightly white, and very tight-lipped,' Madeleine recalls, 'and said that you couldn't believe that I was wearing it and that it was quite awful.'

Philippa, on the other hand, vividly remembers how devastated she felt when her mother turned up wearing it, and how much the dress clashed with her mother's auburn hair.

Even with the passage of time, you see, some things never change. Madeleine's recollection of the dress is of it being very 'toned down' and 'tasteful', while Philippa still shudders at the thought of the colour, the red hair and all those dots.

Philippa virtually banned her mother from the sports day, telling her if she was going to come she had to stay in the background and not be seen by anybody. Of course, Madeleine couldn't not attend at all, because the humiliation of not having one's mother present would be even greater than having a mother wandering around in an unspeakable dress.

Ah, the trials and tribulations of childhood. A teenager at the time, Philippa just wanted in that desperate, aching teenage way to fit in. And how, exactly, was that going to happen with a mother in a polka-dot dress?

With the benefit of hindsight, Philippa feels that perhaps she was, to use a technical term, 'a bit of a cow'.

Madeleine agrees.

Still, if it's not one thing, then it's certainly another. Apart from 'unsuitable' clothing, the other thing that Philippa remembers with horror is Madeleine turning up to collect her in their old clapped-out Cortina with an ostentatiously noisy exhaust.

'It always rattled like crazy, and you'd come up the drive to pick me up from school and it would be roaring, and sometimes clattering on the drive,' Philippa says. 'You're looking quizzical, but I know it's true. I was so sensitive about that car – I'd almost ask you not to come up the drive.'

Madeleine remembers that Philippa hated their Land Rover too: 'You thought that was a disgusting farmery-type vehicle – loud and rough and earthy.'

Either way, Philippa felt her mother made her 'stick out', when she all she wanted to do was to melt into the background.

Philippa also remembers that her mother would always be late to pick her up during lambing or calving, and would leave a message with the teachers that she was 'tied up with the vet'. Previously humourless teachers found this very funny. Madeleine's lateness seemed to Philippa a statement that her mother didn't care, and then she'd compound things by arriving in wellies smelling of sheep.

Oh, the mortification.

Madeleine, like every mother, knows that that most teenage daughters are embarrassed by their mothers' appearance at some point, and feels able to brush Philippa's criticisms off as hormonal and pubescent. However, she does concede that most daughters don't have the smelly business of lambing to contend with.

Back when King Zog of Albania – not the most popular of monarchs – was travelling around Europe in a futile attempt to promote a more positive image of himself, Zogina Ziegler's father, a journalist, covered the story for the English leg of the tour. He found one of the King's daughters very attractive (there's no record of what he thought of the King), and in honour of the attachment he decided that, should he ever have a son of his own, he would call him Zog. But, as you're about to see, he went a bit further than that . . .

A Sprog Called Zog
Zogina Ziegler, 2001

Zogina Ziegler – a mouthful of a name if ever there was one – tells the story of her father's quest to name a child – any child it would appear – Zog. It began when he became godfather to his brother's child. Somehow he convinced his brother that the baby should bear the name Zog. It was only when they got to the church that the full enormity of naming his son after so unpopular a ruler struck the brother. No doubt he could actually imagine tying the millstone around the innocent baby's neck as he lay there wide-eyed and trusting. And so the boy was duly christened Anthony.

It might have interested Anthony to learn that *zogu* – from which 'Zog' is abbreviated – is in fact Albanian for 'hawk': a prouder, more noble association than might have been imagined. Anyway, let's get back to Zogina's father . . .

Because, as the proverb states, if at first you don't succeed, try, try again. And Zogina's father was nothing if not determined. When he married and his wife became pregnant, he knew he had found the opportunity he so craved, with no one likely to frustrate his plans. Except that the son he anticipated turned out to be a girl. But, as you've probably surmised, that hitch was adeptly overcome: Zogina. And in due course another child was born, and he became Zog.

Pleased as punch, Zogina's father wrote post-haste to King Zog to let him know he'd named his children after him. The news – understandably if you were Europe's least popular monarch – appealed to the King.

'My brother received a gold pen and pencil,' says Zogina – spoiling the effect by adding, 'they turned out to be tin.'

Which might go some way to explaining why Zog was so unpopular in the first place.

However, Zogina still proudly wears her gift, a little gold pendant. She remembers the Christmas cards and letters the King would send. 'He'd write inside, "To Zog and Zogina, from Zog" – then, in brackets, "King".'

Sadly, neither Zogina nor her brother, met King Zog. But occasionally their names induced interesting behaviour in others.

'At a party with my brother,' recalls Zogina, 'I was introduced as Zogina. The woman behind me was a bit tiddly, and I heard her say, "That's the Queen of Albania." "The King's kicking around here somewhere too," I wanted to add. I felt very regal. Every time I caught her eye, she dropped a little curtsy.

Sadly, Zogina's brother has decided to give the name a miss with his son, as if reflecting the fortunes of Zog himself (who died in 1961 in case you were wondering). Zogina has no children to name either Zog or Zogina, but she does own a shop, called Ziegler's Ornamental Garden Statuary – or ZOGS for short.

Picture this: a vegetarian sister, her husband and two children move in temporarily with a bachelor brother, a keen meat-eater, who loves fishing, ferreting and hunting for rabbits with his Harris hawk . . .

The Hardest Moment
Eddie Thorne, 2002

Caught in a house-buying chain, and finding themselves homeless, Catherine and her family were kindly taken in for two weeks by Catherine's brother, Eddie Thorne. Two months later they moved out again. The intervening eight weeks were memorable for both parties.

'It leads to one or two interesting conflicts of interest when you have a single meat-eating man and a squeamish vegetarian sister, along with her children, in the house,' admitted Eddie.

The main battleground was the fridge. Eddie's hawk, Henrietta, was fed on a diet that made Catherine blanch. Opening the door to the fridge, she was greeted with the sight of a deep-frozen massacre. Inside were quail, day-old baby chicks, rabbits and rats – all ready to be defrosted for Henrietta to enjoy.

'It's perfectly natural!' explained Eddie.

A vegetarian doesn't necessarily see it that way. But a compromise was found. 'Catherine had to be warned when she could and couldn't enter the kitchen, and containers in the fridge were sealed with "Hawk Food" written very clearly on them.'

The sofa got in the firing line too. Within an hour of the Williams family arriving on Eddie's doorstep, felt-tip-pen marks appeared on Eddie's cream sofa. Desperately amassing half a dozen cleaning products, Catherine worked through them all to get the marks out before Eddie saw the damage. Her work was thorough: not only did she eradicate the stains, she also removed the original colour of the sofa.

But for Catherine the biggest hurdle was hygiene. Permanently attached to an antiseptic wipe herself, it was her brother's preparation of meat that had her hair standing on end. 'Eddie had this chopping board on which he cut up the dead animals. I think he washed it once a week – and that was a concession!'

Eddie's hardest moment came when he returned from holiday: 'I came back to a house still full of kids, with no definite end in sight. All my beer had been drunk by my brother-in-law and replaced by my sister – with food!'

But before he'd left he'd made Catherine responsible for his two ferrets, Lady and Butch, in spite of her protests that 'They're vicious! They bite!' In fact she coped so well that Eddie, who'd been a little concerned about the arrangement, came back to the 'biggest, fattest, roundest, rolliest ferrets you've ever seen! They'd been well looked after.'

Catherine and Eddie even survived the battleground that is Other People's Children. Eddie thought his sister a bit soft: 'She's a very liberal mother . . .' But he was also finding out how demanding it was to be permanently responsible for children – all day, all night; no break – and no sloping off home to his bachelor pad when he'd had enough. Because they were in his bachelor pad.

Eventually the Williamses moved into their new house. Eddie was left alone in his home. 'I took a deep breath, I looked around me, and even for a bachelor there was a fair amount of housework done that day.'

It could have been a disaster, but it wasn't. Eddie and Catherine got to know each other again, and learn about each other's lives, and as a result it's brought them closer.

Would Eddie repeat the experience, though?

'I'd have no objections to doing it again,' he said. 'But I would point out that my brother has an equally large house . . .'

Catherine Williams may have hated dodging the chopped
rats and diced voles that were a part of the tapestry of her
brother Eddie's life. Still, she should be thankful she didn't
have Steward Ellet as a sibling. He didn't even like being a
father to his own children. Who knows what he'd have made
of someone else's?

Grudging Dad
Steward Ellet, 2002

'It was a nightmare really – an absolute nightmare,' Steward
says, reflecting in understated fashion on fatherhood. Don't get
him wrong though. Steward says that he does love his children:
he just realized early on that it was a mistake to have had them.

But it's not their fault.

He says he didn't neglect or ignore them, and took them out
to places, and did all the things he felt he was supposed to do.
But he found being a father utterly boring and not at all enjoy-
able. Steward thinks that many parents are 'living a lie' and
don't really enjoy their children.

Steward was nineteen and his wife just seventeen when
they decided to have children, mainly because it 'was one of
those things you just did'. He feels now, with hindsight, that
perhaps they should have had some life together first.

His son was born when Steward was away in the army, so
he didn't see him until he was three-and-a-half months old.

'From the day of seeing him, there was nothing there.'

Not the usual response of a new father confronting his son
and heir for the first time.

He felt the same after the birth of his daughter a year later,
and had a vasectomy at twenty-two. Steward is nothing if not
consistent, and has always joked with his children about his
attitude, and told them frankly that he's not interested in ever
seeing any grandchildren.

'Close, in a distant way' is how Steward characterizes his relationship with his children now. And he's pretty relaxed about not particularly wanting to see them. There have been the odd moments when they've made him laugh, but overall his attitude to parenting is 'Thank God that's over.'

Steward has never shied away from telling people about his attitude to fatherhood. His colleagues at work know, and, although most claim not to understand him, he says that some tell him privately that they wish they hadn't had children, while giving a different view in public.

He's glad his children have done well, but 'I'll be honest with you. With hindsight, I would never have had children. Never, never. No doubts about it at all. I just wouldn't hesitate to say that – even though I love my children.'

Adrian Mourby, the paternal ying to Steward Ellet's yang, took his two children to the world's most romantic city, to feed their imaginations and their stomachs with the sort of food they could never have imagined. Unfortunately, among his greatest discoveries was that challenging children's taste buds might be too much of a holiday adventure.

My Brain Tells Me What to Eat!
Adrian Mourby, 1998

Picture the scene: breakfast.

'Venice,' Adrian exclaims breathlessly. 'What parent wouldn't want to introduce his children to the delights of European living? I brought my two to a hotel famous for its comfort and its seafood. Yes, I know what you're thinking: "How will seven-year-old John and ten-year-old Miranda react to a plate full of squid?"'

At least breakfast shouldn't pose too much of a problem . . .

'It looks like strawberry juice,' John says suspiciously.

'Why is that?'

'Because it's red!'

'It says orange on the side, but this is red orange juice,' Adrian explains. 'Prune – it's a dried fruit. Would you like to try that?'

'Yuck! I hate fruit!'

Seven-year-old boys are not known for their epicurean adventurousness. Maybe ten-year-old Miranda can be persuaded to eat something a touch more sophisticated.

'Prosciutto. It's a very thin ham. Tell me what you think of it?'

'It's OK, but I think I prefer Coco Pops.'

Lunch.

'John, do you know what this is?'

'Octopus, I can guess.'

'Do you think octopus tastes nice?'

'I don't think I would trust it.'

'But do you think you could try being an octopus-eater just for me?'

'No thanks, it's my brain that tells me what to eat.'

'So what does your brain tell you to eat?'

'It tells me to eat vegetables and meat. It doesn't tell me to eat octopus.'

'So what does it tell you to eat in Venice?'

'It tells me to eat spaghetti bolognaise.'

Dinner.

'We're going the wrong way. McDonald's is that way,' Miranda helpfully points out.

'McDonald's. Do we want to eat in McDonald's in Venice?'

'Yes we do!' they cry in unison.

'Oh, the shame of it!' Adrian laments. 'Am I the only parent to suffer this way? After some investigation I found that, no matter where you go or where you come from, children don't like what they don't know.'

Finally, back at the hotel – where the waiter has bent the chef's ear to suit the English palate. The verdict on the Italian-style fish finger?

'Well, it's fish in breadcrumbs,' Miranda says cautiously. 'And the fish isn't actually cod. But the chips are very nice, and so is the tomato ketchup. So I would say that this is the kind of food that makes you feel at home!'

In our next story, children of a different age present an anxious father with a slightly bigger problem than eating octopus. Anthony Peregrine lives in the South of France with his teenage daughter – who has just discovered the local boys . . .

My Daughter's Dating . . .
Anthony Peregrine, 1998

Life's being good to Anthony and his family this month. The sun has shone, the National Front has won no new seats, and the bloke whose garden borders Anthony's has finally moved his chickens.

'This has allowed my daughter and a couple of her friends to do their revision for upcoming exams in the shade of the trees,' Anthony explains. 'But it also contains the germ of a problem. Sometime today my daughter will announce quite casually, "We've finished Europe 1921–32, so we'll be going out tonight."'

Nights in France start late. Anthony's daughter leaves around ten thirty for a village festival or a disco in town. Not long ago she'd have been satisfied with a meal in a fast-food restaurant. Now all she wants from Dad is a key left under the mat. Anthony has always considered himself a groovy kind of dad, and doesn't want to cramp his daughter's style. But, then again, he's aware what a wild world it is out there. In particular, he's aware of just how demented young men can be around seventeen-year-old girls.

'I myself was always charm itself with girls' parents. I brought flowers, and discussed pottery, politics and the fuel consumption of the Ford Zodiac. I lapped up their family photo albums. Yet, when out of the parental ambit, the fires burned fast and foolish.'

When, obliquely, Anthony mentioned this to his daughter, she replied, 'Don't be silly, I know all that. It's no problem. And, by the way, I've finished Europe. I'll be going out tonight.'

Anthony considers that he may have underestimated her. 'Seventeen-year-old girls probably take all this in their stride. The ones I tangled with batted me off without much trouble.'

Nonetheless, he still calls after her, 'Not too late now – you've still got your exams.'

Even the grooviest dad remains a dad.

Our next story is of a very different experience of parenthood. Fiona Wilson is the parent of a disabled child. Charles has Down's syndrome, which led Fiona initially to reject him when he was born. But a year later she has come to terms with his condition, and her own feelings.

Me and My Baby
Fiona Wilson, 2003

Fiona knew there was something wrong with Charles as soon as he was born.

'He didn't cry, he was purple, he was all hunched up. He was actually very ugly,' she says, remembering the birth.

Fiona was fortunate in that her midwife was also a friend and very upfront about the fact that Charles had Down's syndrome. The way you are told your child has Down's can seriously affect the way you feel about that child for the rest of your life. But, still, for the first twenty-four hours Fiona couldn't hold Charles. She couldn't breastfeed him either. One of the aspects of Down's children is their lack of muscle control, and Charles was unable to suckle.

Fiona and her partner Adam's first reaction was one of complete shock. Their dream of a beautiful bouncing boy had been completely shattered, and they now had to face the prospect that Charles might not even be able to walk or talk. They couldn't understand why their child had been born with Down's, when all the tests during pregnancy had been negative.

But what followed was concern.

'When we're ninety, who on earth is going to look after this child?' Fiona worried.

Nonetheless, her primary concern was for her daughter, Ella-Rose. Fiona's initial reaction was that they were leaving Ella with a burden for the rest of her life. Adam already had experience of the effects of disability on siblings. His brother had been born handicapped, so he knew how horrendous things can be for disabled children and their families.

Fiona's mother's initial reaction probably didn't help either. She found the situation very difficult to accept, although she has since changed her mind. She is in her mid-seventies, and Down's syndrome babies of her generation were put in a home. For six weeks she couldn't look at Charles, and blamed Fiona. She also told her that Ella-Rose's life had been ruined. Her advice to Fiona was to leave her son in the hospital. But Fiona refused.

It has taken a year to get over it. Fiona realizes that none of this was Charles's fault. The situation has also been greatly helped by Charles being such a loving baby. Fiona now sees him as 'adorable'. He makes everyone who comes into contact with him feel special, all of which has helped Fiona to accept him.

There are still testing times ahead for Fiona and Adam. Charles is growing from an infant into a toddler, and they still don't know whether he will ever be able to walk and talk.

But Fiona says that it's already clear that Charles has her stubborn streak. He's a fighter.

'Society's going to have to accept him, and it's just going to have to accept he's different from other people.'

Jasvinder comes from a Sikh family in Derby, and is the second youngest sister of seven. There is one brother. Just over twenty years ago, when she was fifteen, her parents told Jasvinder that a marriage had been arranged for her. She can hardly have been surprised by this, as all five of her older sisters had had a husband chosen for them.

Forced Marriage
Jasvinder Sanghera, 2004

'I watched my sisters being shipped off to India to get married, and they were like sixteen years old,' Jasvinder recalls. 'And I remember when they were married at least three of them experienced domestic violence and issues that were quite horrific, and my family would go there – not to bring her back but to get her to stay there, because of the community's way of thinking; because of what so and so's going to say. So they would always leave her there. And I remember leaving thinking, "Weren't we meant to bring her back and help her?"'

All of Jasvinder's sisters were married in India but then

returned to the United Kingdom, so she had plenty of experience of what was in store for her. However, it was when the fifth daughter was married off, aged fourteen – being removed from school in the process – that the reality really hit home.

'They would make comments about it being my turn. And when I was fifteen they took it for granted that I would do as they said. And then they presented me with a photograph and told me that this is the man that I'm going to be marrying. And I looked at the picture and conjured up all the images in my mind of my sisters and the misery of their marriages and I said to my mum, "No, Mum, I want to finish school. I want to go to college. I want to go to university. I don't want to get married." And immediately she said, "No. You're no different to any of the others, so you will get married."'

Jasvinder – like her sisters before her – had led an astonishingly sheltered existence until then. Chaperoned to and from school, she never socialized, and even a trip to the corner shop required the presence of her brother as guard. Of course, she never had boyfriends.

Her friends were all from the Sikh community, and, while Jasvinder assumes they led equally restrictive lives, it was something no one ever talked about.

'I believe they were caught up in the same system, but you never really talked about it, if you know what I mean. We were the ones that went to school in our trousers, to cover our legs, and we didn't engage in conversations with the other girls when they were talking about going out with boyfriends. We just kept a distance. And I suppose that's part of why we hung around together – because we couldn't identify with what the other girls were doing.'

Although she accepts that arranged marriages can and have worked for many, Jasvinder rejected the use of coercion. However, her refusal to accept the husband chosen for her was at first not treated seriously by those around her. As her mother had said, what made her think she was different?

'Initially they kind of joked with me and said, "Oh yes, you know you don't know what you're saying" and whatever. And then, as I persisted, I was at some points locked in my room. I was chaperoned more so – everywhere with my mum and my sister. And I'd met a very good friend of mine, an Asian young girl, and her brother became a friend of mine – not boyfriend/girlfriend type, but more of a friend to offload on to. So I said, "Mum, I'm seeing somebody." And that was the worst thing I could ever have done, because as soon as I said that they arranged the flights and everything for me to leave.'

In an attempt to undermine her family's plans, Jasvinder took an overdose. But even that couldn't derail them. Instead of taking her to hospital, they simply laughed in her face – making it clear that nothing would stop the marriage back in India that had been planned for her. So Jasvinder changed tack.

'In the end I decided that if I agreed to it while I planned something then this oppressive behaviour would change, and that enabled me to pursue my friendship with this man. And one night, at three o'clock in the morning – it sounds like a romantic fairytale, but it wasn't – I lowered my suitcases from the bathroom window into the garden, and he came and took my suitcases. And from that moment on we started planning the escape.'

Gradually, and as unobtrusively as possible, Jasvinder was trying to remove her life from the family home. But then one day she saw the dress that she was to wear at her wedding, and the enormity of it compelled her to a rasher course of action.

'I saw the dress, everything – all the commotion in terms of organizing this wedding. So one day I saw the front door open, and I just ran in what I was standing in and I ended up at where this person works. I sat on the wall for a good two or three hours, and he came out and I said to him, "You have to help me now – right now."'

In doing so, Jasvinder's friend was taking a considerable risk – not just from reprisals within their own community, but also from the police if the family accused him of abducting their fifteen-year-old daughter. But he did it anyway. The two of them put a pin in a map and it landed in Newcastle, so that was where they went, sleeping rough in his car for a few days before moving into a bedsit.

Three weeks after that, there was a knock at the door. 'A police officer! I just totally broke down, and I explained to the officer the reason why I'd left and I said I hadn't been taken here against my will – this man has helped me. I explained everything. And to my surprise this officer said, "Look, I understand what you're going through and I see this all the time." And he said, "I'm not going to tell your parents where you are, but I will tell them that you've contacted us and you've told us that you're safe." Because I was going to be sixteen in a matter of weeks. And that's what he said.'

Jasvinder was lucky, but she wasn't happy. Despite what they planned for her, she missed her family. She was, after all, a sixteen-year-old girl in a strange city, away from her parents for the first time in her life.

'I begged my parents – ringing them endlessly to say, "Can I come home? Please can I come home?" she remembers. 'And they said, "Well, if you come home you have to marry that person." And I said, "But that's why I left." And they said, "Well, if you don't come home for that reason you've shamed us. Don't ever contact us again. We will treat you as a daughter that has died." I did that for three and a half years. I was extremely depressed. It was as if my childhood had been aborted.'

Her sisters wouldn't call her, because of the risk it would put them under and the effect it would have on their position in the community – although in the end her youngest sister did speak to her in secret. It fell to this sister to marry the man Jasvinder had refused to marry – she had to honour the agreement her family had made. But the marriage didn't work, and ended in divorce.

Jasvinder married the man she ran away with, who – because he was Asian – wasn't blamed for helping her. Aged twenty-three, they returned to Derby, to a reaction she never imagined.

'When I came back to Derby, when I was older, people on the streets often came up to me and were shocked to see me because they believed that I had died.'

And for reasons you would never wish for.

'My sister had committed suicide – the one just older than me. She did on several occasions come back to the family and beg for help, and was always told to go back, because of the family name and honour. And she set herself on fire. She suffered 80 per cent burns. This death-by-fire idea is almost an honourable way to kill yourself – rather do that than make an independent decision and live your life and totally disgrace the family. When she died, I thought, "This is never going to change." And I just thought, "I'm not going to sit here waiting for them to accept me any more. I'm going to go back." Because Derby was always home.'

Jasvinder and her parents did start to talk again – but always in secret, for fear of the shame the communication would bring upon the family. But the rest of her family still refuse to talk to her, crossing the road if they see her in the street.

'People say to me, "Do you feel you've betrayed your family as an Asian woman?"'Jasvinder says. 'But I feel that they betrayed me. I feel my mother betrayed me as a daughter, and my family have as a sister. I understand that my parents were holding on to some traditions, steadfast traditions, in Britain. But when it becomes a situation of force – and I was beaten and locked up in a room – if they couldn't see that that was wrong then they betrayed me. And I do blame them for not putting their hand out to me during that time.'

In 1994 Jasvinder set up a shelter for women in a similar predicament, and it's always full – supporting some forty women a month. To many in her community, Jasvinder was again dishonouring her traditions and throwing down a gauntlet to the status quo.

'Initially, when we started the project, in the first two years we used to get death threats; we used to get phone calls left on our answerphone: we'd get letters. But it just made me more determined. I'm known as the woman with no shame.'

Moreover, she's a mother herself now – to a nineteen-year-old girl – and living proof that some traditions do die.

'As long as the individual respects her as a human being, she can marry black, white, Asian.'

Helen has cared for her thirteen-year-old granddaughter Cindy all her life. (These are not their real names.) Her granddaughter knows there's nothing Nana wouldn't do for her, and there's not much she wouldn't do for Nana. This is just as well, because, when they talked to Home Truths, *the pair were enduring one of life's lows – living in a hostel for the homeless. Here they recall happier times, and reveal an indomitable optimism about the future.*

Nana and Cindy
Helen and Cindy, 2000

'My favourite memories are when my kids were little and seeing them grow up and get married,' Helen recalls. 'The biggest thing of all was when I saw my eldest granddaughter married – on my birthday. There were over three hundred guests, and the best man got them all to stand up to wish me happy birthday.'

Cindy's favourite memories revolve around Christmas: 'My Nana invited some of the family round, and she had got me a camera and I got a picture of my granddad washing up – and Nana just laughed and laughed and laughed. It was just so funny.'

Cindy has lived with Helen since she was born. Her mother's inability to cope with her meant that, when Cindy was three, Helen got a court order to ensure she remained her guardian until Cindy was eighteen.

'My relationship with my daughter's not happy,' Helen explains. 'She's got married again, and had another baby, who's now up for adoption. I'd take her home, but they wouldn't let me take any more. They weren't looking at my age. They were looking at the two major operations I'd had for cancer of the bowel. They thought it was too much for me to take on another one. I told Cindy she was a very lucky girl! We've had our problems. She's carried on like all kids do, but at the bottom of it she knows if I hadn't taken her she'd have been where her sister is.'

'I do love my mum,' Cindy says. 'But I love my Nana more than anything. I love her more than my mum. My mum brought me into this world, but my Nana's been there for me. She's gone through the bad stages with me, and I never used to think I could talk to my Nana, because she was my Nana, but I can talk to my Nana about anything. I can say anything to her, and she's always got the answer.

'When we first came here we felt weird,' Cindy continues, talking about the hostel. 'We're not used to being in a hostel. We're used to being in a house. We're used to being at home, watching TV, sitting down and having a good old family chat.

It's been hard for us both, trying to get used to things, but I suppose sometimes it's got to come.'

'Let's put it this way,' Helen says pragmatically. 'It's a roof over your head, and somewhere to put your head down, and somewhere to be safe. Whereas, if I was roaming around, I wouldn't have anywhere. They've been good to me. But it's just the rules! For Cindy – well, kids don't seem to bother as much as us with the rules. She can't do what she wants, and I had to pull her down a bit and explain to her that she's got to abide by these rules. She says, "Nana, let it not be long before we can get a house, so that we can be together – we can get on with our lives without anyone breathing down our necks."'

'I hope someday my Nana's dream will come true,' Cindy continues – 'just to get out of here. And touch wood she don't die in a place like this. I want her to die at home with all her family round her bed. She was in hospital last year with cancer. She's scared she's got cancer somewhere else. I hope she hasn't. Most of all I miss my family and my baby sister, who got put into care last year. And it's been hard for us both, because they won't let me and my Nana see her.'

'But we did speak to a social worker,' Helen counters. 'And the people who have taken her are not going to let her forget she's got a Nana and a sister who still love her. I feel bitter, because I can't do what I want to do – much as I want to. It hasn't been easy, but, as I say, I love her to bits, and I won't let anybody harm her. I'm a stubborn woman. I'm determined I'll pull through, and that Cindy and I will get a home where we can live our lives and get on with it. What I want now is for her to get into school, keep her education up, so that she can do something useful with it.'

To which Cindy replies, 'I want to be a school nursery teacher, and the best mum that any kid could ever have, and for my Nana to see me grow up. I want her to see me grow up. If I could have one wish now, it would be for all our family to get on with each other, and all of our family to be in their rightful places and with their rightful parents. But most of all it would be to have my sister home with me. I wish it every night, but it never seems to come true.'

Stumped for a name for their firstborn son, Heather and her husband took inspiration from an unusual quarter...

Naming the Kids
Heather Harper, 2000

Heather is a rational, rather upper-class-sounding mother of two sons, who are are twenty-two and twenty-four years of age. All quite normal – until that is, Heather reveals her sons' names. Then all of a sudden things don't look quite so normal any more.

'The elder is Heston Kenneth Plowright Harper, and the younger Toddington Warwick Harper,' she says firmly, going on to explain, 'My husband and I just couldn't agree on a name for Heston – not Harry or Charlie or anything. As we drove from the nursing home in Wimbledon back home to Iver, in Buckinghamshire, we started calling out all the names as we went along – Roehampton, Putney. But on the M4 we still didn't have a name, so we called out any name we could see – even the offices we passed: Siemens, Honeywell. Literally the exit before home was the Heston service station. I said, "Great! Sir Heston Harper sounds brilliant!"'

In retrospect Heston seems to have got off lightly, given what he could have been called. In fact he is actually quite pleased with his name.

'He said every time he goes for a job interview, they remember him,' Heather explains. She goes on with what she insists is a true story: 'A lot of people associate his name with Charlton Heston. A friend of mine was the theatre manager of the Savoy, where Charlton Heston was appearing. I said, "Go on, get an autograph for me and tell him my son was named after him." My friend did just that, but Charlton Heston said, "I bet he wasn't named after me. I bet it was that service station on the M4!"

To call one son after a motorway service station might be overlooked. But two? Heather has a perfectly rational-sounding explanation for naming her second-born Toddington.

'A friend of mine said, "If you've called your first son after the first service station on the M4, how about calling your second son after the service station on the M1 – Toddington?" "Great," I said, "it's got a lovely ring to it."'

4

Loss

In its time, Home Truths *broadcast stories of heartbreaking sadness, frequently recounted with a minimum of fuss and little sentimentality.*

But first take a deep breath and relax, which is exactly what Sue Jenkins thought she was going to be able to do in 2003, when, eight years into a happy marriage with Norman, she gave up the pressures of teaching art with a view to becoming a student once again. Casting about for an idea on which to build an MA project, she finally alighted on her own family.

Filming the End
Sue Jenkins, 2005

Sue had been teaching in further and higher education for many years. However, she was an artist, and she found that she had stopped doing her own work because her time had stopped being her own.

'You're lesson-planning or reading up on lectures,' she says. 'So I decided the best way to change this would be to do another qualification.'

So Sue enrolled on the MA programme.

'And then, of course, you have to find a subject – what you are going to study. You have to put a proposal in. So I went through all my artwork with a friend of mine, and she was really helpful because she helped me to see that in my artwork the woes of my life were laid out before me – this was when this was wrong; this was when that was wrong. And we had this chat about what I was going to do next. And she made a wonderful comment: she said, "You know, Sue, the problem with you now is your life is trouble-free. You're really quite middle class, aren't you?" And it really struck a chord, because looking at the artwork you could see all the traumas of my life laid out. So anyway I put the proposal in – basically looking at art as a testimony.'

One of the things that movitated Sue's proposal was the memory of her mother burning all her father's photographs when he died. He was a keen amateur photographer, with a huge collection. Wherever he went his camera went, and all his spare time was spent in the darkroom.

'I've tried to speak to her about it, and I kind of get the feeling that she just hated the fact that he spent all his time with the photographs and not with her. It was kind of like "Well, I've lost all that time, and these are the objects that I'm going to vent the anger on." She doesn't regret doing it. She just did it and then got on with life – which was quite strange to witness.'

This experience made Sue want to explore what made a person act that way, because she felt at the time that everything her father owned was precious, a piece of him. And yet there was his wife destroying the one thing that he really had a passion about.

'So I really wanted to look at grief, and how it makes us react in various ways.'

Sue's choice was to prove bitterly ironic: 'I'm my own case study.'

Norman, her husband, had been suffering from back pains. Too late, they were diagnosed as a rare and fatal form of lung cancer. Understandably, Sue tried at once to pull out of her project. But her tutor, Gordon, was having none of it. Matter of factly, he told her to buy a digital video camera and record anything and everything as it occurred. When Sue refused, Norman himself stepped in to convince her.

'I really did not want to go on with the MA,' she says. 'I mean, we were told not to look past Christmas, and this was in September. And I really didn't want to waste time being away from him. But he was adamant that I would carry on, and in hindsight I can see that he really needed to see me do something. He really needed to see that I was looking beyond the situation that we were in. I think for Norman it was him watching me carrying on with life and in a way putting something in place that would ensure that I carried on.

'And it was really great, because we went and bought this digital video camera, and neither of us knew one end of a camera from the other,' Sue's voice warms at the memory, 'so this also gave us an opportunity to play together, to read the instructions, make mistakes, have a laugh at what we'd actually done. And he filmed quite a bit himself – I've got somewhere between thirty and forty minutes' footage of Norman just filming the trees with the birds gathering to migrate and then flying off. And in fact that's a good example of how we sometimes don't see what's happening outside of the frame when you look at photographs or film, because I imagine Norman standing there, watching these birds gathering to migrate, and maybe thinking about his own destiny and where his journey was going to take him. I'll never know, because I can't ask him. He also became quite obsessed with putting his shed in order – he sorted all his nails and screws and socket sets and hammers, and I can walk into the shed and everything is labelled.'

It wasn't like that before. Norman really wanted to make sure that after he'd gone, if Sue needed to do any DIY or repairs or anything, she could just go in the shed and find whatever she needed. 'You know: I need a screw of a certain size, I need a bracket, I need a washer – and it's all labelled and laid out there. And he filmed himself doing this – which for me is a really wonderful bit of footage.'

The filming brought them together in other ways too. In the evenings they'd sit and watch the footage and laugh at themselves and how they'd spent their day.

'But there was a real point where Norman realized that he was actually going to die,' Sue remembers. 'He put on a lot of weight, because of the steroids, and we'd been out and bought him a load of clothes, and I was filming him trying on all these clothes and we were having a joke about how for the first time in his life he was quite fashionable and up to date. And when we watched that bit of footage back he turned to me and said, "I'm really sick, aren't I? And I'm going to die." So from watching that he could see himself and the change in himself, and recognize what was happening to him.'

It was at this point that Norman started sorting the shed out and clearing out his personal possessions. 'And I sometimes think if we hadn't used the film and watched that little bit he might not have done all those things that he needed to do to make himself comfortable.'

The doctors gave Norman until Christmas, so he was delighted when he woke up on Boxing Day morning. He died later that day.

He was, Sue says, a very determined man – more a man of action than a talker – and he used his remaining time from the first diagnosis to contact all the people he hadn't been in touch with for ages and to plan his own funeral: a funeral that he insisted should take place with the minimum of fuss. No grieving; no flowers or cards. He didn't even really want anyone in attendance. As hard as that was, Sue felt determined to carry out his wishes, however painful they were for everyone else.

Now he's gone, Sue has the films to remember Norman by.

'Well, he was absolutely right – both Norman and Gordon have been absolutely right. The films have really got me through some desperately dark moments. For the first few months after Norman died I couldn't even bring myself to look at them, and I used to rehearse how I would go into the university and tell Gordon that I wasn't going to do it. And then I would get guilty, because I'd promised Norman that I would carry on. But you know they became a wonderful tool for me. I found that the more I watched, the more I cried, the more I got the emotions out of my system – the anger at him having died and left me; the pain of having lost him. And then I slowly started to edit the films, and more and more saw it as an absolutely fascinating subject and area of study.'

When they started to make these films, neither Sue nor Norman knew what they were doing. But in the sleepless nights after his death Sue found some solace in the user manuals and guidebooks to filming, and she'd while the nights away practising, making mistakes, and trying again.

'So the manuals for the programs that I was using and the trial and error involved in actually editing the films were something that I became completely absorbed in and occupied my time, and I've spent many hours reading through the manuals, not understanding a single word. I mean, the program kept asking me would I like to insert a slug – which didn't seem like a good idea to me at the time, and in honesty doesn't seem like a good idea to me now. It was quite some time before I discovered exactly what a slug is. It's just a blank bit of screen.'

Sue wasn't sure she wanted to show the films to anyone. Although not harrowing in themselves, they were acutely personal. Gordon, her tutor, encouraged her to exhibit them in the degree show – an act, like so many since she started the project, which produced results she never expected.

'I exhibited in the end-of-year show. And the best thing to come out of having exhibited them is that Norman's friends came on the opening night. Because he hadn't had a funeral they hadn't had a chance to actually say goodbye to him, and they commented on the fact that they felt like they were at Norman's funeral service – that they were really thankful that I'd given them the opportunity to get together and laugh about Norman and grieve and cry as a group of friends. So that was something I hadn't anticipated.'

And, for the record, Sue got her MA.

How do you cope when your grief for the death of your husband becomes front-page news, and every private moment becomes public?

Grieving in Public
Janine Goss, 2001

Janine Goss's husband, Mick, died in 1996 after the helicopter he was piloting crashed on the way back from a football match in Lancashire. On board were four other men, including Matthew Harding, Chelsea Football Club's vice-chairman and a high-profile businessman. Within hours of the crash, journalists were on to the story, eager to discover more about Harding's complicated private life and his final moments during that fatal trip. Already trying to cope with their personal tragedy, Janine and her two sons (then aged eleven and five) found themselves at the centre of a breaking news story in which they were, at best, bit players.

'Until it happened to me, I always imagined when news broke that the next of kin knew that their nearest and dearest had been killed in an accident,' Janine says. 'I found out on the breakfast-television news.'

It was Janine's eldest son, in the middle of getting ready for school, who shouted to his mum that there had been a helicopter crash. Realizing what had happened, Janine rang the local police station, demanding that a police officer come over to be with her and the children, despite the receptionist's insistence that Janine was overreacting.

Tabloid interest in their story began almost immediately after Janine had her husband's death confirmed. 'The policeman with me picked up the phone, thinking it would be a colleague, and it was a tabloid journalist wanting details. The policeman told them their phone call was very inappropriate.'

This didn't deter the press at all. Within half an hour they were camped outside the house, forcing Janine and her sons – all extremely distressed – to leave their cottage by the back door to maintain their privacy.

Janine had to keep the curtains closed against the long-range camera lenses.

'The children were just so upset. My youngest son, only five at the time, curled himself up into a ball and didn't want to talk to anyone. He kept saying over and over, "Why have they got cameras on our house, Mummy?"'

The press, of course, remained inured to the pain they were causing the Goss family. Janine had to deal with frequent phone calls asking for comments, and her neighbours were constantly harassed.

'Many of my neighbours weren't even aware that Mick was a helicopter pilot, and certainly weren't aware that he'd died,' Janine says. 'They all felt the intrusion to be totally inappropriate. One elderly couple came to me in tears, saying they were really sorry: they'd spoken to the press, and the story didn't actually say what they had said.'

Even at the funeral the television cameras were present. The press intrusion made grieving difficult for the boys and Janine, especially as Janine's father died four days after Mick.

'He had lung cancer, but his prognosis was good. I just feel the shock killed him.'

Two years later, when the story was out of everyone's minds, Janine decided to move. But the press were still watching her, reporting that she was moving because she had debts to pay, which was a complete fabrication. The pain was compounded by the threat of legal action by the Harding family, on the grounds of possible negligence on Mick's part.

'I could understand them wanting to get compensation for Matthew Harding's loss of earnings, but it was the fact they were trying to prove Mick negligent when he was just doing his job,' Janine remembers. Having her dead husband besmirched hurt enough, but there was also a real financial threat: if Mick was proved to have been negligent, half of his estate would have been taken, which would have left Janine and the boys homeless. Fortunately it didn't come to that.

A year later an inquest took place, and once again Janine had to endure the media spotlight and the press's love of hyperbole. 'During the inquest, the coroner asked me if I would like to leave the court when they played Mick's last communication from Air Traffic. I said yes, and someone sat in a room with me, and took me back after it had been played. The following day the coroner looked to the press and said he was disgusted that they had reported that I had fled from the court hysterically.'

Several years on, the problem still hasn't gone away. When the jockey Frankie Dettori was involved in an air crash, the press were back banging on Janine's door.

Time should be a healer, and Janine and the boys are doing their best to put those years behind them, remembering Mick for the loving husband and father he was. Grieving is a painful process for anyone, but for Janine there is the dread of the media's unrelenting interest to contend with. For them, her husband's death is an opportunity to fill space, and every time a helicopter crashes, or there's a problem with a plane, they're on the phone or at the door. Janine will never forget Mick, but she wishes the press would.

Losing a parent, a partner or a family member is never less than devastating; it's always going to be like losing a limb. People say, 'You'll get over it.' But a dull phantom aching, where a part of you has gone for ever, does always remain. Sometimes accidents of timing can add a further cruel twist to grief.

Jo-Anne Mason's mother died following a long illness. Unbelievably, Jo-Anne's partner Frank's mother also passed away on the same day. This double blow had a crippling effect on their relationship.

Jo-Anne's Mum
Jo-Anne Mason, 2004

'I knew from the previous evening that she'd got very, very weak,' Jo-Anne Mason sets the scene. 'And then I had a phone call from my father, and he just said, "Can you just get round here quick now, Jo?" Which I did. And as we got there she died. So peaceful – it was just like she'd just fallen asleep.'

Before this the mother of Jo-Anne's partner, Frank, had been in good health – rude health in fact. But in the week leading up to the death of Jo-Anne's mother she started to suffer from high blood pressure and palpitations and she was rushed into hospital.

'They said, "Well, nothing to worry about. We'll just give her some medication and things and we'll calm her down." On the Thursday night we left the hospital after seeing Frank's mum. She was sat up, cheerful, feeling a lot better.

She said, "I'm feeling better now. I'm even looking forward to having my hair done in the morning." And we thought, "Well, she must be feeling a bit better."'

When her mum passed away, Jo-Anne felt that at least they had Frank's mother left, someone they could share. But – with a sense of timing that seemed to belong to a Greek tragedy – the phone rang almost the moment she and Frank walked back into the house. It was the hospital calling to say that Frank's mother had passed away too.

'And I just . . . I was just absolutely dumbfounded. I said, "No, she can't have." And it was literally within an hour. And I thought, "Well, what's the likelihood of this ever happening to anybody in a million years?"'

Organizing one funeral is traumatic and draining enough. But two . . . One might imagine that Jo-Anne and Frank would provide solace for each other, each knowing what the other was going through. But that wasn't the case.

'No, we weren't a comfort to each other at all,' Jo-Anne says. 'At the time that my mum had been poorly, on occasions when I'd been looking after my mum, I'd come home and I used to break down in tears, because I didn't want to cry in front of my mum. I think you tend to put a brave face on and bottle it all up, and by the time I used to get home sometimes at night, after being with my mum, I used to burst into floods of tears. And he used to say to me, "Don't be so soft. What are you being so soft for? What are you crying for?" But suddenly the shoe was on the other foot. He hadn't been prepared for it at all – I don't think he ever thought it was ever going to happen to him. But you see it did, and so it was a case of his grief was greater than mine. You know?'

The funerals, and all they entailed, proved all-consuming for Jo-Anne and Frank. Once they were over, however, the couple just started arguing, the bitterness pouring out in shouting and screaming fits. In the end Frank returned to his mother's house, to the little box room, which his mother hadn't changed since his childhood.

Jo-Anne, abandoned, mourning her mother, slid into depression. She left her job, and felt her moods just grow blacker and blacker.

'I thought, "Well, I've just had enough of everything" at this point. I just went into a very, very deep depression, which was just this blackness. Obviously you think, "Well, I can't carry on like this." And then I went to the doctor, and the doctor prescribed me some medication, which I felt worse taking. And I thought a lot about when I was a little girl and the little simple things in life that had made me happy,' Jo-Anne remembers. 'They were simple things like walking and I was brought up near a farm and I used to go haymaking and doing things like that – back to nature. I thought, "I've got to go back to the beginning here, and I've got to get out and start looking at things again."'

Ultimately, and perhaps surprisingly, there were two things that helped Jo-Anne clamber out of her despond. The first was getting a dog. Well, two in fact. She'd always wanted a Jack Russell, but she couldn't make her mind up when she saw the puppies. And, of course, when she had the puppies she had to walk them, so she literally had no choice but to leave the house.

'And I heard also a particular piece of music that just changed things for me completely. I can remember being upstairs in bed this particular day – didn't want to get up, didn't want to do anything – and this particular piece of music came on, and it just described the way I felt . . .

'It was Goreski's Symphony No 3. There was pain and there was this sorrow, and then suddenly as the music changed everything just became fresh and new and I felt this warmth all around me, and it was just as if my mum was there. And I just felt it envelop me. It was the most incredible feeling that I've ever experienced in my life. I felt she was there with me in the room, and she was saying "Everything's fine now and I'm at peace and it's time now, Jo, for you to move on. No more crying. No more sorrow. Please, just move on now and get on with your life." And I did.'

Jo-Anne and Frank were still living with their separate griefs, although they communicated with short phone calls and little notes. Then Frank decided to sell his mother's house – to move on too, presumably. And with that decision came another one: he didn't want to be alone any more.

But things weren't the same as before. How could they be?

'When he came back I was happy for him to be back, and he was happy to be with me. But I can honestly say everything changed around, and I became his mother.'

Jo-Anne asked Frank to contribute to her story for *Home Truths*, and at first he agreed – which thrilled Jo-Anne, because finally she'd hear his side of things. But in the end he decided he couldn't do it. Frank was a big, strong man at six foot two. And talking about, let alone showing, his emotions, was something he was conditioned not to do. Nonetheless, despite this setback Jo-Anne continued to put her life back together.

'I just got it into my head I wanted to learn about computers, so I enrolled myself on a little absolute beginners' course doing computers, and it gave me something to focus on – something new and something fresh. And in between walking my dogs I also got an allotment, and started to grow vegetables. I bought some chickens and I had a few free-range eggs and things like this. And in between going on my allotment and digging and everything I read more books on computing. And I thought, "If I put my mind to this I could teach. I'd love to be able to teach this." So that's what I did.

'Out of all that blackness and darkness and thinking "Will I ever feel happy again?" I've just seemed able to turn everything around and have a fresh start. It was definitely cathartic for me.'

Nick and Jo McCann had expected that 1999 would be their first Christmas as parents. But that January, their daughter was stillborn . . .

A Stillbirth
Nick and Jo McCann, 1999

Jo was thirty-nine weeks pregnant, just a week away from her due date, when she became worried by the complete stillness of the baby she was carrying. Concerned, she phoned her friend who was also the midwife who was to deliver their baby. She advised Jo and her husband, Nick, to go to the hospital for a check-up.

Even before the news was broken to them by the doctor, Jo and Nick knew that the worst had happened. 'You could just tell by the looks on people's faces. That was the worst moment, realizing yourself that the baby had died,' Jo says.

Her initial thought was 'I want a Caesarean, now!' But her friend took her and Nick home.

'The worst night of my life,' Nick remembers.

However, when the couple returned to hospital the next day to have the baby induced, Nick didn't find it a traumatic experience. 'When she was born, she just looked like any other baby,' he says.

Nick and Jo named their daughter Agnes Mary.

Talking to other women about the experience, Jo finds that most assume that giving birth to a dead baby was the worst aspect of what had happened to them. 'But actually it was quite wonderful,' she says, her voice straining with the memory, with the rawness of the emotions she felt despite her child being dead.

'You hold on to things as time goes on,' Nick says, agreeing with her. 'And you realize at that moment what love is. The intensity of it is what stays with me – that depth of feeling that you'd do anything to have Agnes back. It's not a negative thing at all. Sad, but not negative.'

The McCanns had a room to themselves, and spent much of the day following the birth with their daughter. Jo describes the enlightened approach of the hospital staff towards their situation: they helped the couple take photographs, prints of Agnes's feet and hands, and a lock of her hair.

Nick found it hard to return to his work as a primary school teacher, but, trusting in the maturity of the eleven-year-old children he teaches, he talked openly to them about what had happened.

'The letters we had from the children were the best creative writing they did last year, because they were totally from the heart,' he says.

Initially this helped, but Nick admits that he was deflecting his feelings in taking on a traditional, male, supportive role. He immersed himself in work, but as the school wound down for the summer break the death of his daughter hit him, and he had the long summer holidays with nothing to do but dwell on Agnes Mary.

Nick found himself grieving for the relationship he had not had. 'Jo firmly believes that Agnes had nearly forty wonderful weeks being very cosy and very warm. The woman gets the chance to build that relationship. I think it's a sad thing that the man doesn't get the chance to build that relationship until the baby's born. But that's a fact of life.'

Jo and Nick are considering having children again but both feel it might be wiser to wait for a time, until they feel better able to deal with what they both know will be an anxious nine months. Coming to terms with the death of Agnes has been painful, and continues to be so, but both of them have found a strength in each other and in their relationship which has helped them cope with the devastation and sadness of their loss.

In 1999 Steve Hammond, then aged twenty-one, became severely ill with schizophrenia, and life in the Hammond household changed dramatically. His parents, Terry and Chris, had both worked for many years in mental health services, so were probably better prepared than most families might have been. Nevertheless, they were hard hit by the emotional upheaval of it all.

Steve
Terry Hammond, 2004

'He was actually a really gentle lad,' Terry says, recalling the time before Steve was ill. 'He was fairly introvert, but he was quite a sporty lad. Not an academic, but a very practical kid and a very likeable kid – he had lots of friends. Your average child really.'

Steve went to college, where he learned the painting-and-decorating trade. He was also a good artist and a pretty skilful footballer.

It was during his time at college that his parents began to notice the changes. 'He started to go to college late, and Steve had always been a child that was meticulous about time – he used to tell me off when I got him to school late,' Terry remembers. 'But he started sleeping in, he started smoking heavy, and he started staying in his room, which was really unusual for him. He started to become a bit of a recluse. And I was saying to Steve, "I really think you should go to the doctor's. I think you're getting depressed."

'But then it really all happened in a very short period – the actual psychosis, if you like, came out very quickly. I came home from work one day and was sitting having my dinner when Steve looked me in the eye and said, "Why have you rung the BBC?" And I said, "What do you mean, Steve?" He said, "Well, they've been broadcasting that I'm a lazy bugger all day." And my heart fell. I just then realized he was actually a very seriously ill young man.'

According to Terry, Steve had always been quite a vulnerable person, an anxious child, and that may well have contributed to his psychosis.

'But Steve has got no doubt that cannabis was the thing that triggered it off, because he was bingeing on it because he thought it was safe and he preferred it to alcohol, to filling up his stomach with beer,' Terry says. 'He says it was after an incident in a nightclub where he ran out of paper, so he ate a piece of the resin. He passed out, and when he woke up he heard voices saying, "It's OK, Steve, you can get up now. You're OK." And they were voices in his head, and he's had them ever since. So there's no doubt in my mind and in his mind that cannabis was the thing that triggered it off.

'You know you can't say it caused it, because it's a very complex – I mean, the human brain's very complex. And you know he was potentially a vulnerable personality, as there are something like about one in ten or so of us have got so-called vulnerable personalities.'

Terry and Chris, understandably, found Steve's illness enormously difficult to deal with, despite their professional backgrounds. They had to confront their sadness over the son who had disappeared with the onset of the psychosis as well as contending with the illness itself.

'It was very, very hard – particularly before he went into

hospital, which was about a month. I mean, Steve basically was shouting, and he'd be pacing about in the middle of the night. Basically you're dealing with a man who'd lost complete control of his thoughts.'

Steve was never violent, except with himself. Frightened to death, he would bang his fists on the door and bash his head against the walls, screaming for the voices to go away.

'He was terrified at buses going by,' Terry says, 'because he was convinced that the people were hearing him. You couldn't talk to him. You couldn't rationalize with him.'

Steve thought he'd been taken over by aliens. 'He said to me, "How else can people get in my head like they are?" To show you how powerful the voices are, when the doctor said to him, "Where do you think they're coming from?" he said, "Well, I think they're probably coming from within my head." And the doctor said, "Well, how certain are you?" Steve said, "Well, about 88 per cent." The doctor said, "Well, what's the 12 per cent?" Steve said, "Well, the 12 per cent, it's the things my voices say. They're so clever sometimes – I can never ever think of things like that."'

Eventually Steve calmed down, and it seems the voices calmed down with him. They were even telling him jokes. 'And I used to say, "Well, Steve, perhaps you're a comic genius,"' Terry says. '"Because", I said, "if they make you laugh as much as that . . ." And he's slowly getting better on that basis. But occasionally they catch him out.'

Steve was sectioned and put on anti-psychotic drugs to stabilize the brain chemistry for around three months. When he came out he was much more in control of his thinking. But the voices remained, and they're still with him now.

'We went to the theatre not that long ago,' Terry says, remembering a time when the voices made their presence felt. 'And I said, "You will control your voices, Steve?" He said, "Oh yeah, absolutely." And as soon as the curtain opened he made some remark that he hadn't intended, and he said, "Oh, Dad, I'm going to have to go – my voices are playing me up a bit.'"

It took two years of cognitive therapy for Steve to learn to be able to distinguish and control the voices in his head. The therapy helped him understand that aliens hadn't been invading his brain, but once he had regained some of that control he still had to find a way to reconnect with the world around him.

'I've got some really great friends and I've got a great daughter who deliberately take him out and get him integrated to do what we need to do to rebuild him basically – rebuild his confidence and self-esteem.

'You know, I take him down the pub and his voices unfortunately manifest in a way that he actually speaks his inner thoughts. We went into a pub and a really nice young girl sat down beside us, and he looked at the young girl, he looked her straight in the eye, and I won't say exactly what he did say but it was to the effect that "I would really like to make love to you." But he said it in a perhaps bit more descriptive way. The young girl was obviously horrified. Her partner, who was six foot six, jumped up and was about to hit him, and I jumped in between and said, "I'm ever so sorry, Steve's had an accident. He's got brain damage." And they backed off.'

When Terry asked Steve if he realized what he had just done he said no. He had *thought* it, yes, but he had no recollection of actually *saying* it. Steve was mortified.

Ever since Steve's illness, Terry and Chris have felt huge conflicts over how to treat him with other people and how to explain their son to those he meets. Steve's sister, Victoria, first had to confront the situation when she was studying at college, which was hard enough. Then there was the procession of boyfriends who had to have Steve's condition explained to them. One of them never came back. And such situations and the attendant dilemmas continue. They feel an obligation to warn people about Steve's illness, but at the same time they feel as if they're betraying him by doing so.

'You're really caught there, I mean about one's respect for the individual. But I do warn people in the main,' Terry says, explaining the decisions they take. 'And Steve is quite up front about it. I mean, it's been four years now, and so . . . The one thing that was a bit sad about it was when he did actually realize that actually it was an illness, that it wasn't aliens: he did sort of say to me, "Am I really this ill, Dad?" and "Do you think I'm going to be like this for the rest of my life?"'

The answer, Terry believes, is no. Steve will learn to live with his illness, and it will improve. He may not be cured, but over the last four years Steve has slowly but surely learned to manage his condition.

'It's a bit like people who lose the use of their legs, or people with diabetes,' Terry says. 'You have to manage it and learn to live with it. And obviously mental illness is a bit more difficult, because it affects your whole being. It affects who you are.'

It's easy to see how committed Terry is to his son's recuperation and care. But this effort and love has been very demanding of his time, and of Terry and Chris as a couple. Their life together has effectively been put on hold.

'We were in our early fifties and we were great – looking forward to the kids flying the nest and rediscovering ourselves again. And I used to joke with Victoria that I'm going to grab everything that Saga can throw at me. But in fact that's all been put on hold. And on a practical level it can be quite difficult because Steve smokes incessantly and we're non-smokers. And there's also that guilt when we do go away for a weekend that Steve's at home, or Steve's with Victoria.'

Terry and Chris have taken Steve away on holiday, but the flights are a nightmare because Steve can't smoke on the plane, and without cigarettes he's likely to – and does – start to hear the voices again. But the humour and resilience that have obviously helped Terry, Chris and Steve handle the last four years emerge once again when Terry describes how they overcame that particular hurdle. 'We stuck patches all over him. He looked like he'd had an accident he had so many patches over him.'

Twenty-eight years ago, J. P. Devlin was a twelve-year-old schoolboy and summers lasted for ever . . .

Childhood Sweetheart
J. P. Devlin, 2005

'My last day at primary school fell in June 1977. It was a happy day. Master Higgins let us play outside for most of the afternoon before calling the whole school together to wish us all the best for the two-month summer holiday. He reserved some special words for us, the class of P7. It was the first time we had to deal with leaving people who'd been a huge part of our lives. The thing was that only a few of us had passed the eleven-plus and I was particularly saddened that my best friend, Shane, had failed. Shane and I wouldn't be going to the same school any more.'

As Master Higgins continued his delivery J. P. glanced over to Regina Gates. He caught her eye, and she gave him a cheeky wink and a smile. He continued to watch her as she listened on – long dark hair and rosy red cheeks, and that sort of face that smiles so brightly that you could barely see her eyes when she beamed from ear to ear. She had passed the eleven-plus too, and he was so glad that he'd see her again.

J. P. spent the summer out on the road helping his father make his deliveries to shops, travelling around towns and countryside in his two-ton lorry, pulling in at one o'clock to listen to the news and eat tomato sandwiches.

'I would stare at the vista afforded from sitting so high up in the cab of a lorry and daydream about Regina Gates,' J. P. remembers. 'Every evening we would return down the steep hill towards our house, to be greeted without fail by my younger sisters, who would run the length of the garden waving to welcome us home and then with great speed and excitement splutter the latest news, which they had gathered while sitting open-mouthed in our kitchen as visitors popped in.'

And so it continued.

By mid-August J. P. had his new school uniform. But then he heard the awful news. 'Regina Gates had been knocked off her bike by a car and was in hospital. Every day after that I couldn't wait to get home, coming down that hill with my sisters waving each evening – learning more about how Regina was. But I knew that something must be wrong when after a week she was still in hospital and there had been no change.'

Now, twenty-eight years later John Devlin and his sister are standing in the garden that she used to run down with the day's news as she remembers Regina's story.

'I remember that summer being very, very hot. I think summers back then were very hot – anyway, they seemed to be. And we'd all wait – you could always hear the lorry at the top of the hill. That particular evening we had news – big news. So Sian, I remember, ran down the garden to the wall shouting, "Stop. Stop the lorry." But Daddy always stopped and let John off at the gate anyway. And he got out, and I remember us all shouting, "Regina Gates is dead. Regina Gates is dead." John didn't have much reaction. He just stood there. He didn't move for ages – he just stood there staring at us.'

'I felt my stomach fall out of my body,' J. P. responds. 'I had to be strong – I was the eldest, after all. I didn't want to cry in front of my sisters. I didn't want to make them cry. But most importantly, as an eleven-year-old boy, I didn't want anyone to know that I had been in love with a girl. I couldn't admit to anyone that this was the saddest moment I had ever known.'

His sister remembered that he just didn't react at all. 'You just got out of the van, jumped down, heard what we said, and didn't have any reaction. You didn't have any reaction. You just stood there – just stood still.'

J. P. never actually knew how seriously Regina had been injured. His mother just told him it was some wee thing that went wrong while she was asleep, and that's the image he kept – 'Her sleeping serenely on a hospital bed of white linen, with Lucozade and grapes on the bedside table. It's an August night, and some wee thing goes wrong and she passes quietly and unknowingly into heaven – where it was decreed by all the adults she would certainly be heading.'

Almost thirty years later he still thinks about Regina, and doesn't want to forget about her. For years J. P. visited her grave – not just because she's there, but so that she knows he still remembers.

'As the rest of her classmates grew into adults, her parents must have thought their daughter would be just a distant memory for us,' J. P. ponders. 'I wanted to visit them and say it was a terrible thing that happened. I wanted to tell them that someone else was thinking of her. I promised myself I'd make that visit.'

'Well, here I am now at Regina's grave and just looking at the headstone, and it reads, "In loving memory of Regina Mary Gates who died 23rd August 1977 aged 12 years." And etched now on the grey marble are the names of her parents,' J. P. continues.

He thinks it was probably for the best he didn't meet her parents. In his mind she has actually grown old with him, her image in a strange way timeless, ageless.

'And I don't know how I'd have felt if perhaps they'd shown me a photograph of a girl aged twelve. Maybe too they would have found it strange to hear from me after many years. Such a sad thing it is for a child to die – my childhood sweetheart, who had that sort of face that smiled so brightly that you could barely see her eyes when she beamed from ear to ear.'

5

You Couldn't Make it Up

One of the defining qualities of Home Truths *was the truly bizarre quality of some of the stories – from obsessions with coffins to welly phobia and electrically heated underwear. Truth really is stranger than fiction.*

Those who work on canals have traditionally considered themselves at least the equals of those more celebrated voyagers who ran with the Trades or did battle with a giant squid in the turbid waters off Tierra del Fuego. Indeed, in some respects the narrowboaters were the braver, for, while the sea folk had beacons and buoys to light their passage, the canal folk had nothing to guide them but a ragged towpath and an asthmatic horse. Until recently that is. For Phil Austin has built a lighthouse forty miles from the sea on a tricky bend in the Bridgewater Canal. He did this entirely off his own bat, without a penny from Trinity House. Why?

Lighthouse Man
Phil Austin, 2005

Nearly eight years ago Phil Austin was living on a narrowboat on the Bridgewater Canal, an experience which was his introduction to the world of canals and canal boats and the culture and lifestyle of those who owned and lived on them. Eventually Phil bought his mooring and the land around it.

The question was: what to build on the land? The planning department explained that, as Phil was living in a conservation area, he'd need to build something appropriate and sympathetic to the surroundings – no Portakabins or caravans, and nothing made out of wood. And all the while Phil was thinking, in a sniggery sort of way, 'What about a lighthouse?' But he didn't just act unilaterally: he talked to his neighbour on the next boat – Alex – who, instead of saying, 'You're mad,' said, 'What a great idea.' So basically it's all Alex's fault.

In keeping with the time-honoured role of lighthouses, Phil built his on a bend on the canal – as a warning to approaching boats, so it's not just a folly.

'My first discussion with the planners was very tentative,' Phil admits. 'I kept talking about a storage building. "Oh yes. Tell us more about it." I said, "Well, it'll probably be about three or four storeys high." And they said, "Whoa, whoa – it's only a small piece of land." I said, "Well, it's only going to be a small building. It won't have a big footprint."'

No. Instead it will have a narrow, round footprint.

'I was reluctant to mention the word "lighthouse", because I didn't want to be laughed at. But in the end he said, "I can't quite picture it." I said, "Well, to be honest it's going to be a lighthouse,"' Phil continues. 'And there was a pause, and he said, "You're breaking up – are you on your mobile?" I said, "Yes, I am." He said, "Well, can you park somewhere, because you're breaking up, I thought you said 'lighthouse'." He genuinely thought it was a mobile breaking up.'

But it was made of stone, and tangentially appropriate. Well, not stone exactly – 'Concrete blocks,' Phil clarifies. 'I did consider stone, but it was far too expensive. So I worked out a way . . . In fact I had a chat with poor dear departed Fred Dibnah about it. I rang him up one day, and he was on the phone for about half an hour – I couldn't get off. But he was telling me how they used to build the old chimneys and stuff, and he said, "Concrete blocks will be fine.""

So, Phil built his lighthouse – with an unerring verisimilitude to an actual lighthouse, except it's completely landlocked. It's thirty-six feet tall, with a Tardis-type room for three or four people to sit in and look out. It also has a walkway around it, just as all good lighthouses do, and on top there's a beacon rescued from an old lightship in Truro. And the light does work – if Phil turns on the switch.

Living on the narrowboat allowed Phil to save enough money to buy a flat. Not that he spent long there, because when he met Jan he moved in with her. Of course, sharing with Jan freed up a considerable amount of money – which Phil spent on building the lighthouse.

Jan was more understanding than you might expect any person would be. And it did keep him occupied – not least trying to overcome the bane of all lighthouse keepers' lives: how to get square furniture into a round room.

Phil illustrates the problem: 'I went to Ikea and asked for the lighthouse section. And of course they're never going to make money, because they just don't cater for lighthouses.' Although it wouldn't take a huge leap of imagination to picture the Svern or Wave range, would it?

So Phil is making his own. Because not only does he own the lighthouse that's probably furthest inland, he also owns the only one that's manned.

And if that's not romantic, then what is?

Simon used to work in the music business as a lighting engineer. When he decided to move on, he became a postman – a job he really loved. But reorganization and the move to a single delivery per day meant staff cuts, and, as he was one of the last ones in, Simon was one of the first ones out.

Fortunately for us, Simon used his six months or so in the Post Office well.

The Postman
Simon, 2004

'I enjoyed the early mornings,' Simon told us – 'the being out and about, working on your feet. There are two parts to being a postman. The first part is you're indoors sorting the mail for your particular delivery area – the six or seven streets – and you're faced with a mound of unsorted stuff, which you have to compartmentalize in this big frame in front of you within a certain time limit. And then', he adds in a slightly regretful tone, 'you bag it all up in a logical order and then you sort of undo everything you've just done by putting it through everyone's letterboxes. And hopefully at the end of the day, at the end of your allotted six-hour shift, or whatever it happens to be, you've got all the relevant letters into the relevant holes in the wall and everyone's happy. And then the job's over – you don't have to think about it again until the next morning.'

As the new kid on the block, Simon got one of the longest rounds – nearly three hours. Time, for an observant fellow like Simon, to notice some of the amusing and incongruous things that life threw up.

'You're given a privileged position of trust, in a way, in being a postman,' Simon remarked, 'in that you know everybody in that area, in that street and the adjoining streets, by name. And some of the names you couldn't make them up. It just started with Tracy Lacy – though what's amusing to me wouldn't necessarily be amusing to anybody else.'

Well, a sense of humour is a very personal thing. But it's nice to know – reassuring even – that somewhere on the face of the earth there is a person called Tracy Lacy.

'Precisely. And there's someone called Bertha Day. And

Bernadette Frisby, Janice Buttery, Lisa Jelly, Jasper Litaferber –' Simon was warming to his task now – 'Rachelle Le Love. Bentley Videl was a good one.'

It sounds as if Simon had a round populated by the weirdly named. But, as he explained, he'd visit nearly four hundred homes in a postal round, and he did ten or twelve rounds during his time as a postman. So probably, and rather sadly, there weren't that many extraordinary names. They're just the ones he savoured.

And then there were the people with quite normal names, except that someone else had had them first: Julie Andrews, Richard Burton *and* Elizabeth Taylor, and James Bond. Not to mention the incongruities that only a postman might alight upon as he pulled the envelopes from his sack.

'There was a Mr Rainbow who lived two doors down from Mr Flood. And somebody called A. Seaman lives two doors from C. Waters. And Mr Woodcock and Mr Partridge living very close to each other. And the Moodys living opposite the Jollys.'

And no doubt it could go on.

Here's a story after Simon's own heart. There was much musing on Home Truths *about names, inspired by the question: is there a Dot Com? Apparently, there is – in California. This news was relayed by one Gervase Markham. Gervase Markham? A pretty unusual name in itself, you might think. Clearly not, however, because here are two: grandfather and grandson.*

Meet Gervase Markham
Gervase and Gervase Markham, 2000

The Revd Canon Gervase (it's pronounced 'Gerviss') W. Markham, MBE, MA, is ninety years old and lives in a small village in Cumbria. His lifestyle, however, is far from that of a retired clergyman: he speaks roughly twenty languages, plays croquet, runs a huge camp of choristers every summer, and arranged for a fifty-ton granite millennium monument and a pop festival last year. His name has been in the family for several hundred years, and, conscious of the preceding generations, he calls himself Gervase Markham V.

'And I always sign myself Gervase W. Markham. And my grandson I call or write to as Gervase R.'

His energy is boundless. According to his grandson, he's still gardening and building walls – on his own. 'He'll ask me to give a hand with a particularly heavy stone, but normally he's tossing the rocks around like there's no tomorrow. Absolutely amazing,' Gervase R. says.

The Markhams have been around for generations, four of them as sheriffs of Nottingham and one as a favourite of Elizabeth I. The most famous was Gervase the author. 'Two of his more famous books are *Cheap and Good Husbandry* and *The English Housewife*. A lot of his books are made up of household hints he collected from various farmers' wives. He'd no idea whether they were any good, so half his stuff is really good and half is complete rubbish,' Gervase R. explains.

He too has displayed the Markhams' flinty, entrepreneurial spirit. 'I did manage to flog water I'd bottled from the spring here to the entire village. I bought a bike from the proceeds. The sign of a good entrepreneur is someone who can sell something which people should be able to get for free!'

The Markhams, it seems, are never at a loss. When Gervase Markham V retired from being a vicar, he set himself a challenge stiff enough to make lesser men blanch: 'I wanted to read all the great books of the world in their original language. I started with the easy ones, Homer and Virgil.'

He's worked his way through Dante in Italian and *Don Quixote* in Spanish, and is currently studying Russian with *War and Peace* as his next objective. He's also happy to recite the New Testament in Greek – in a modern Greek accent, of course.

On the face of it, the old-fashioned scholar who has no computer or wireless and his dot-com whizz-kid of a grandson may seem worlds apart, but there is an oddly similar quality about them. Is it the Gervase gene?

A journey prefaces our next tale, albeit a pretty short one: to the newsagents to buy Viz *and then back again. No chance of Ian Wood winding up on the way to South Africa like Helen Wingate Marsh. He just walked down the road, and then walked home. So what's so unusual about Ian's story, then?*

Leaving Home at Forty
Ian Wood, 2003

'It says a lot that I'm still buying *Viz* as a forty-year-old. A few other things I did as a boy which I still do now, despite being more than halfway past my allotted three-score years and ten: I still love liquorice allsorts, still love *Thunderbirds*, and still go to, erm, pop concerts. I saw Britney Spears once. 'You rock, Birmingham!' she yelled. 'And so do you, Britney,' I thought. No one else my age at that gig thought so, but I'm pretty sure the children they chaperoned did. One other thing I do which I did as a boy: I'm still in the parental home.'

But not it transpires for much longer. Despite being forty, Ian still has a good relationship with his parents – which is handy. And if his friends think he's strange they don't say so. Ian, however, recognizes the peculiarity of his position, even if it's taken a while to sink in.

He explains the genesis of his stay-at-home existence: 'Aged nineteen I left for polytechnic, but my home was too close for me to qualify for seven-day accommodation, and I had to return home at weekends. There was no real incentive to learn to cook, iron, do laundry, keep an orderly property or cope with household bills.'

Ten years ago Ian had a taste of independent living when a friend went travelling and asked him to look after the room he shared in a large house. 'This was close to the kind of character-building domestic regime I'd opted out of as a student. But it was not a happy time – with bills, cooking, cleaning. I scurried back to an option that protected me from financial pressures and domestic obligations.'

The eccentric hours Ian works mean he can go almost a week without seeing his parents. To their great credit, they've never accused him of treating home like a hotel – even though he does. 'They'll be delighted to see me settled in my own place, but never have they put pressure on me to leave.'

His parents, Ian observed, are in the British vanguard of a European trend for children to remain at home until they find a partner. He didn't comment on whether they rejoiced at their pioneering role or not. And it could be that staying at home is a form of rebellion against the money-hungry property-ownership ladder – a new form of counter-culture, with three square meals and darned socks.

'That said,' Ian continues, 'My parents have signalled their intention to leave the city where I was born and brought up, and I've signalled my intention to stay here. I'm going to face the gamble millions of others face every year in leaving home for good. The risk goes beyond the financial. It'll test my personal resources: the ability to organize a smooth-running household, to do everything that's always been done for me, to have friends round for sophisticated dinner parties and not be fazed by the responsibility. I could just buy somewhere near a McDonald's so that'd solve that problem.'

Remember, Ian, you said sophisticated dinner parties.

The choice to leave home will be the first of hundreds that

Ian is steeling himself to face. Which mortgage? What kind of property? What kind of decoration and furniture? Whether to have a garden? Or a lodger to help with the bills?

'But,' he says, 'for all the decisions that lie ahead, there's one I'll have no trouble making. I will not, under any circumstances, watch a television makeover programme.'

When Richard Bunn retired, some fifteen years ago, he decided he needed an absorbing hobby to keep him occupied and active. He considered golf, gardening, fishing and so on, but they all seemed somehow fatuous, banal – pointless even. He wanted something with a bit more gravitas.

So he started collecting Asda supermarkets. But not in the way Wal-Mart has. All he wanted to do was 'bag' them, the way some people bag mountain peaks or pubs with legs in their names. So far he's visited all but one of the 265 stores, which sounds like a dead end. But with new stores opening all the time there seems little chance of him having the full trolley for long.

Asda Man
Richard Bunn, 2004

'Well, it all started fifteen years ago, when I retired from business life and wanted to think up a means to continue to get myself around the country and visiting places. I could have collected National Trusts or Boots or Marks & Spencers, but at that time when we lived in Northampton it was convenient to take the dog for a walk in the forest near Corby, then go on to the Asda at Corby and have an all day breakfast, do the shopping, and then fill up with petrol and drive home.'

Collecting Boots or Marks & Spencers would have been

ridiculous, clearly. And now that Richard has put his hobby into that broader context it all starts to make sense.

'And that went on for two or three years,' he continues. 'And then I realized that they had other stores in other parts of the country, and the whole thing mushroomed. We used to take short breaks and holidays in a particular area, so that I could comb that area.'

As far as we know, Asda don't have too many stores in Tuscany or the French Riviera, so just exactly where did Richard go?

'The furthest distance is Elgin, north of Inverness. When Asda actually realized that I was doing this stupid activity on my own, they sponsored a trip doing the twelve stores north of Glasgow and Edinburgh.'

This turned Richard into something of a celebrity in the world of Asda. He spent a day in Govern being photographed and interviewed, and in return Asda paid for his petrol and bed and breakfast for the journey to Elgin.

Sylvia – that's Richard's wife – sometimes joins him on these trips to the north of the land and stays in bed and breakfasts, so she obviously doesn't think he's gone completely mad.

'Well, it was our sixtieth wedding anniversary last week, so she's had plenty of experience of me being off my rocker. In fact this is the lesser of my hobbies. I've collected two thousand Nat West service tills, but that's taken twenty years to do those. Subconsciously, this is why I started on Asda, because Asda predominantly had Nat West tills in their premises.'

So now we know. What sounded like an eccentric pastime is now revealed to have a sneaky logic to it: Richard could bag an Asda and NatWest service till *at the same time*. But how does anyone know he's been there?

'Well, I've got receipts – I have valid receipts. Or I did at the very beginning. The trouble is, though, after fifteen years the early receipts started to fade, so I had to revisit and get more up-to-date ones.'

When Richard started, Asda was a smaller, more manageable, family-run business. But it's not the sheer number of shops now that presents him with the greatest obstacle. It's the lack of a store restaurant. Over the years they've eased them out, but after driving twenty miles to get to the supermarket Richard is ready for a cup of coffee. So now he's making other arrangements . . .

'If there's not an Asda in the area and there's a Morrison's, I use the Morrison's,' Richard says.

And as if the decline in coffee shops weren't enough, Richard doesn't even get a discount in Asda, despite his fealty to the chain. 'I've never got a discount, to be perfectly honest. In fact that's another nail in their coffin. Originally they used to give you a discount on petrol, but they don't any more. But Morrison's do, so . . .'

As a shopper, however, Richard is much more even-handed. 'We also shop in Tesco's and Sainsbury's and Safeways, and probably Somerfields. You name them, we've been to them all – to make comparisons.'

Despite an attitude to shopping which some might view as a bit fast and loose, Asda have asked Richard to open one of their stores – in Basildon. But now he's mentioned Morrisons so favourably he might get the invitation withdrawn.

Then again, those are the risks you take when you embark on such an adventure, Richard Bunn. And they say Chris Bonnington is an inspiration to youth . . .

Journeys of a different kind now – but arguably just as eccentric as Richard Bunn's pilgrimage to every Asda in the land.

Derek Parker commutes ninety-odd miles so that George Rowe can cut his hair, as he has done for forty years. That's well over a thousand haircuts.

Enduring Ritual
Derek Parker, 2002

Derek Parker makes a 180-mile round trip to have a haircut. That's because he lives in Darlington and George Rowe, his barber, lives in Hull. Derek has been having his hair cut by George for forty years. Wherever he's been living, he's made the trek to Hull.

Over the years the two have become good friends, and they've come to know each other, and each other's families, very well. Derek's own daughter is a hairdresser, but he won't let her touch his barnet.

George enjoys the fact that Derek is very extrovert and noisy. 'He's the sort of guy that if you come to work in the morning in a bad mood you're glad of him because he just brings you round.'

Derek hates his natural curls, and likes George to cut his hair as short as possible – much as he has done for forty years. 'It's always been a ritual, if you like. It's always been part of my life to have my hair cut, and George has always done it. I suppose it's like getting up in the morning and cleaning your teeth – you just automatically do it, don't you?'

When the two first met Derek was twenty-three and a bricklayer, and George had just done his apprenticeship as a barber. Derek would come off the building site and pedal his bike down to George, who'd then cut his hair. In return, Derek would tidy the salon. Then they'd head off to the Minerva and have a few games of pool – which George always won – and a few drinks.

Derek and George have shared a good deal over the years,

both sad and joyful. 'I think we have a little bit more than just a client–hairdresser relationship,' George explains. 'I think we do feel if we have problems that we can talk to each other. Derek was very supportive when I was having difficulties accepting my father's death. Although Derek is quite outspoken, he's quite sensitive. The same with some of his problems – he's had problems in his life with his marriage. I know when to ask questions and when to shut up.'

Both George and Derek (who's now a publican) find that in their respective jobs people do confide in them, and share intimate details of their lives. And as George points out, 'You get so involved with your clients. The people that come in here are people you've known for many years. Then they lose their partners, and you've that to cope with . . . I've been in positions when I've had to walk out of the shop into the back to mop my eyes.'

Derek Parker's journey in search of the perfect haircut clearly struck a chord. Kate Baynes commutes by Eurostar to visit her hairdresser. But Pippa Courtney-Sutton can trump that: she used to fly out to Spain.

Once you've added in the hotel room and return air fare it's hardly a snip, is it?

Bad Hair Day
Pippa Courtney-Sutton, 2002

When Pippa Courtney-Sutton gave up life on the ocean wave for a shore-based existence, she settled in Mallorca, always having her hair done by Leo. The familiarity made her feel less anxious. 'I'm frightened I'm going to come out looking like an extra from *Star Trek* or something. I've had lots of those sorts of haircut.'

Pippa believes our hair is part of our personality, part of who we are, and that's why walking into a salon and meeting a stranger who is going to cut our hair is such a terrifying experience. It's always distressing coming out of the hairdresser's looking like something that really isn't you. 'A couple of times I've been so upset about it I've come home, looked at it, washed it five times, realized it's not going to change, probably had a few glasses of wine, and set about it with the kitchen scissors,' she explains.

When Pippa came back from Spain, initially she just couldn't face a London salon, so she flew four times a year to Mallorca so that Leo could cut her hair. Part of this was to do with the fact that Leo used to work on yachts as she had done, and that she initially had her hair cut sitting on a sunny dock with a beer in her hand, which made it very different from the terrifying experience of entering a salon.

Finally a friend pointed out that flying all that way for a haircut seemed a little excessive – though Pippa hadn't thought of it that way – and she re-established contact with a hairdresser she had seen some fifteen years before.

As far as Pippa is concerned, getting your hair cut is 'therapy in a way, because if your hair's looking good you feel a lot better, you feel a lot more confident'. Isn't that worth a plane trip?

Alan and Jean Taylor live in a small house on a small island, Orkney. With space at a premium, you'd think they would be wary of clutter. Well, you'd be wrong . . .

Inheritance
Alan and Jean Taylor, 1998

The Taylor residence is small and unaffected, but it is jam-packed with over three thousand bits of china. The Taylors have nearly five hundred teapots – none of which they actually use.

'We have the collection bug,' Jean says with commendable understatement. 'If we see something we like, we just start. There's a bit of competition to see who can buy the most.'

With three thousand pieces, you wonder if it might be time to stop.

'My favourite thing', Jean continues, 'is my chandelier – the dearest thing I've bought.'

It cost £5.

Alan, still shaking his head at the memory of such extravagance, was disgusted she'd spent so much: 'If I pay more than 50p for something, I think I'm being done.' But he does see that his collecting obsession might be an addiction. 'I'm just like an alcoholic or a druggie.'

One surrounded by a legion of porcelain owls.

It might appear statistically unlikely but hugely fortuitous that Alan met Jean, but the collecting bug clearly hasn't proved hereditary. Donna, one of their five children, remembers growing up surrounded by the collections: 'You never touched things. It made me grow up thinking that my house would never be a clutter. I like clear spaces,' she adds – 'nothing lying about.'

And if her parents were to leave their collections to her, what would she do?

'I'd sell the whole lot, quickly – or worse! I'd like to take a rifle to the chickens. I quite like the paperweights and the fish. But the rest . . .'

Alan doesn't seem to mind though. 'I hope when I go I'll come back as a seagull and can fly above them seeing them get rid of all this rubbish! That'll be grand!'

Travelling and journeys seem to be quite a feature of this chapter. But now we turn to a trip of quite a different kind – one the traveller has spent a considerable amount of time imagining and planning, but one she'll never actually experience. Unless, of course, there really is an afterlife . . .

Joan Macarthur's Ashes
Joan Macarthur, 2004

Joan Macarthur from Worcestershire recently read about someone who wanted their ashes firing heavenward in a firework, and decided that that's exactly what she wants to happen to the post-mortem Joan. Husband Malcolm isn't quite so sure.

Joan begins the story: 'Well, we've always roughly said what we are going to do. And then of course I saw this article in the *Saga* magazine with this idea about going up in a firework rocket. And that just grabbed me – I thought that was a great idea.'

Joan, it turns out, has always loved rockets and fireworks.

'I'm one for the unusual,' she continues, 'and I just thought this would be tremendous fun – not for me particularly, but for all those watching. And it would be a great send off – hopefully.'

Joan is lukewarm about burial, and the family don't have a plot; and she's always loathed the idea of cremation. But now she's had this idea she is much more relaxed about it. After all, cremation is just a stage in the process of turning her into a firework.

'I'm quite happy,' Malcolm says, having resigned himself to the event. 'If I'm still about I suppose I'll have to arrange it, so, yes, if that's how she wants to go then I'll arrange it for her.' Personally, he's not too fussed about whether he goes up in a rocket or not. 'The main priority for my funeral is to get a few bottles of malt whiskey and make sure my friends have a good drink. But apart from that I think I might just have my ashes mixed with a bag of bonemeal and plant a tree somewhere.'

So, while Malcolm is nurturing a tree so the planet can breathe, Joan will be hurtling towards the ionosphere – a concept some of her family aren't entirely happy with.

'Well, I think the teenage grandson said, "Well, I'm glad my name's not Macarthur – nobody can associate me with it." Then there was the comment "Well, Mum, we always thought you were crazy. Now we know." The little ones think it's great – so there we are.'

Fireworks are quite a tradition in the Macarthur household. With lots of birthdays in October and November, Malcolm has always organized plenty of displays as a means of celebration. Perhaps it's the resulting familiarity with the varieties, sizes and types of fireworks that has helped Joan and Malcolm maintain such a light-hearted attitude in their planning.

As Joan says, 'We've all got to go sometime.' And, since deciding she's going to go when the blue touchpaper is lit, Joan has investigated the whole firework and funeral relationship in quite some detail.

'Apparently,' she says, 'some firework companies are hoping that all the crematoria in the country are going to be able to provide fireworks for people that need them. So we're thinking of starting Launch a Gran.'

For £1,700, it turns out, Joan can have her ashes put in thirty-six whopper rockets, which would take six hours to set up, and her name would light the sky. Six hours? It's like an Apollo launch. But she's settled for something less grandiose.

'I decided I think I'll go for the £200 job that I've heard about. A portion of your ashes are put in the top capsule of an ordinary firework, as far as I can gather, and that's launched in the usual way. So one of the family will just have to light the touchpaper.'

From hens' eggs, mighty court cases do grow. Anastasia Heath tells us her warning tale . . .

Poached Egg?
Anastasia Heath, 2001

'When I was about seven I owned a hen,' Anastasia remembers. 'She was a Rhode Island Red cross Light Sussex, and her name was Jane. I trained her to go for walks with me, wearing a soft braid harness and a lead. I held a short bamboo cane, and when I wanted her to turn left I pressed gently but firmly with the cane on her right wing; likewise I pressed her left wing to go right.'

One day Anastasia and her hen walked up the village and went into Fryer the Grocer's shop. Yes, yes: fryer, eggs . . .

'Jane paused inside the shop to lay an egg. A fearsome dispute then broke out, because Mr Fryer claimed the egg was his legal property, having been laid in his shop,' Anastasia says – adding resolutely, 'That wasn't at all how I saw things.'

The case failed to reach the High Court, however, because no lawyer could find any precedent.

'My father,' Anastasia says – 'always a prudent man – then took out insurance against any legal costs or damages his children might land him with before we were of age.'

Mr Heath, you could say, definitely wasn't counting his chickens before they'd hatched.

When Michael Simpkins was growing up in Brighton in the mid-1960s there were really only two things he was interested in: eating sweets and playing cricket. Fortunately for Michael his parents had bought a confectioner's shop, which meant an endless supply of sweets, his busy parents never noticing him dipping into the stock. His interest in cricket was inspired by his two elder brothers, who both played the game and went to watch it at the county ground at Hove, which Michael was too young to go to. So, what was a boy to do?

Not Quite Cricket

Michael Simpkins, 2003

'I persuaded my dad to play a form of the game with me in the shop. Most evenings, in between serving customers, he spent the final hour bowling a rubber ball from one end of the shop, just by the display stand for ladies stockings, to where I stood crouched with a tiny bat over by the greetings-cards carousel.'

The shop hardly resembled your typical cricket pitch, so local rules abounded. A gentle tap back to Michael's dad was worth a single, a clean hit against the side of the ice-cream fridge counted as a four, but any shot landing in the chemist's-sundries cabinet was automatically out, as was an injudicious swipe into the cigarette shelves.

'I see now that most of these regulations were attempts by him to dissuade me from systematically destroying the stock,' Michael reflects – 'though I fear it was a forlorn hope. Nonetheless, our game prospered until one evening in late April when I had a greater than usual rush of blood and smote a mighty six back past his outstretched hand and into the Easter window display. The match', Michael comments ruefully, 'was abandoned.'

Which was a great pity, because by now Michael had formed

his ad-hoc cricket games into a league – a sort of John Player league (a reference no doubt lost on some of our younger readers) set among packs of John Player's. He had four teams, bonus points, home and away fixtures, and imaginary players with which to swell the ranks of his imaginary teams.

'After the destruction of the Easter display,' Michael remembers, 'Dad rarely seemed to have time to play again – I think he was worried it was bankrupting the business – and eventually my fantasy players had to pack their bags and move into a new dimension.'

Fortunately, by now Michael had come across a game which most boys of his generation will remember – *Owzthat*, a sort of upmarket dice game consisting of two tiny roller-shaped dice which came in a metal tin, and specially created for boys with imaginary cricket matches and nowhere to play them.

'I spent the next few years sitting at the parlour table pushing the rollers up and down and correlating the runs and wickets in exercise books. Four teams grew to ten, then to sixteen, until I had an entire county championship.

'I kept the league going well into my twenties, often turning to it in times of anxiety or stress – after an unsuccessful job interview, or dumping by a girlfriend,' Michael says. 'It's many years now since I've looked at it, but the players are all up there in the attic, sealed in imaginary aspic within the tiny blue tin and countless exercise books – three hundred-odd individuals patiently waiting for me to open the lid and release their powers once more: demon bowler Anthony Hoathly, gritty opening batsman John Hindfield, Freddy Briggs, Wally Sanderson, Ted Brall, the exotically named Abdul Casinji of Glamorgan, and of course my personal hero, Black Magic.'

In real terms Black Magic must be about seventy now, but suspended in the cocoon of Michael's memory he will still be thirty, still be batting, and still be acknowledging the applause from his loyal supporters sitting watching from the boundary – 'somewhere between ladies' hairnets and the tub of Jameson's Raspberry Ruffles'.

As you can probably imagine, irritating noises is a topic – rather like Haile Selassie spotting – that Home Truths *listeners found fathomlessly fascinating. Can't remember? Well, here's a taste.*

Irritating Noises
Sherie Trotter-Johnson, 2000

'I cannot abide anything repetitive – loud clock ticking being the most obvious example – or "wet" voices,' Sherie says in a tone of voice anything but 'wet'. 'I get very disgruntled at people who don't clear their mouths of excess spit before speaking. I frequently have to turn off the radio and miss part of a particularly interesting interview or some such thing because every other word is squelchy and there's too much half-swallowing going on. Yeuch yeuch yeuch.'

But the worst thing of all is a combination of the two: Baby Maggie from *The Simpsons* being a prime example.

'I quite like the programme, but can't watch it – for days afterwards I have that "suck-suck" noise that she does stuck in my head. It's like water torture waiting for the next one – in fact even thinking about it makes me feel queasy.'

John, Sherie's boyfriend, finds all of this highly amusing. He doesn't seem to suffer from 'suck-sensitivity' at all.

'Surely I can't be the only one,' she muses. 'He also chuckles when I make him put his alarm clock inside the wardrobe because I can't sleep with ticking. I can't read or concentrate to write or do anything really with a ticky clock about. My best friend on the other hand, finds ticking soothing, and has several clocks about her bedroom to help her sleep. She's got to be in a minority, right? Surely I can't be the odd one?'

Tania Bates is a big fan of anything that fits her notion of the contextually inappropriate – like an inland lighthouse, for instance. If you see a beach in a garden, a garden in a living room, a living room on a beach, chances are that Tania will be lurking somewhere nearby. And yet it all started so simply . . .

Life's a Beach
Tania Bates, 2005

'I had a very scrubby front garden,' Tania explains in a tone of voice which suggests that what is to follow is completely matter of fact and day-to-day ordinary. 'A little front garden, with a tiny bit of lawn looking very sorry for itself, north facing. And I thought, "I'll just mulch it out." So I got some sea pebbles and mulched it out.'

Nothing strange about that. Right now there are probably gardeners up and down the land nodding in agreement with Tania's course of action. Pebbles and mulching – seems spot on.

'And then I thought, "Well, I've got some sea pebbles, I'll maybe have a few shells." And I thought, "What I really need is some sand," obviously. So I had half a ton of sand delivered.'

Were the shells or the sand or the half a ton of the stuff the point at which you gardeners thought to yourselves, 'Hello, we're a long way from mulching here.'

'And then I realized that I needed a boat,' Tania continues, in the same straightforward, nothing-amiss-here tone she adopted at the beginning. As if *needing* a boat was the most obvious thing in the world.

'So I got a boat. So the boat kind of comes out of the beach – comes out of the wall. And the downpipe actually forms the mast with the rigging. And then I've got a banana palm and a rather nice palm tree, and of course I finished it off with some tropical-looking kind of foliage and flowers in the summer. And that's my beach.'

Tania, you might be beginning to appreciate, doesn't do things by halves. And, while she is clearly very proud of her creation, one has to wonder what her neighbours made of it all.

'Well, I think initially they weren't too sure. But I think they're quite converted, and in fact I think probably the whole street has become very well known for its colour.'

Not to mention its miles of sandy beach – an unlikely phenomenon in Cardiff.

'We had some South Africans move in. They painted their house bright green, with this fantastic African design. And then somebody painted flowers on one of their houses. So I don't think anyone else is in a position to comment, actually.'

Those of you who like any colour so long as it's white, or who've become addicted to taupe, are probably shuddering at the thought of this multi-hued avenue, but Tania thinks it looks wonderful and colourful, not loud and garish. She also calls it 'contextually inappropriate' – which is one way of describing a street in South Wales with African designs, a boat and a palm tree in it.

'Well, I think "incongruity's" probably a better word, now I think of it,' Tania says thoughtfully. 'And I think it's because incongruity underlies an awful lot of humour. An inland lighthouse is very clever because it's a kind of related incongruity, because of course you do get lighthouses on water, but not on canals. I think that's particularly witty. And you don't really get boats and tropical beaches in gardens in South Wales, so that's obviously incongruous.'

Some of you might be pleased and some might be alarmed to discover that Tania continues her 'contextually inappropriate' theme indoors as well.

'When I was about nineteen or twenty I used to have a room in Balham and a very understanding landlady. And again things tended to snowball.'

Funny that.

'I bought some plastic flowers back from Greece. I thought they were funny because they were tacky, and I ended up turning my room into a garden. And I had Astroturf on the floor. My sister made this wonderful duvet cover with kind of like ponds on and little animals and things, and I had brilliant brick-wall wallpaper and I was making a garden shed for my wardrobe. And, yeah, that was really nice. And then the pièce de résistance I never did but I always wanted to do was to put plastic curtains outside the window and a plastic bunch of flowers outside, because then you would be inside looking outside but it would be reversed.'

Thereby challenging the conventional view of what is in and what is out.

'Oh yes, thank you for that analysis. Absolutely – that's what I meant. Yes, I think it's just challenging the conventional view, entertaining.'

Fans of fine brushwork or those who think painting is real art are probably thinking that if Tania had entered her garden or bedroom for the Turner Prize she'd now be a famous exponent of Brit Art, instead of a mother of one small boy with a lifelong determination to bring some colour and wit into people's lives. Which neatly brings us on to Tania's son. And here I can almost hear your imaginations racing ahead of you. Just how contextually inappropriate was he?

'Well, I'm not really a big baby person. Children are nice, but babies – not really. They're not furry enough in my opinion.'

Or at all, hopefully.

'And I should have really made him furry I suppose, come to think of it,' she adds as an afterthought.

An opportunity missed, an open goal right in front of her, I can hear you all thinking. But fear not. Babies, as Tania quickly divined, have no interest in fashion or in the ramifications of mixing spots and stripes.

'You know, they don't know any better. You can dress them in what you like, can't you?' Tania asked, rhetorically.

Well, up to a point maybe.

'And what I tend to like is kind of quite whacko interesting clothes, and I wear quite a lot of black. So I thought, "I'll get him some black basics, and then they'll co-ordinate with all the other things I'll get him."

Right.

'And you can't buy black baby clothes.' Tania actually sounded surprised. 'You have to buy pastel – it's pastel or nothing. And the more I couldn't buy black baby clothes, the more determined I got to get black clothes – because why not?'

Well, there are probably a few reasons . . .

Tania wasn't going to be frustrated in her desire to deck the mewling infant out like Count Dracula, however. She dyed everything, or imported baby clothes from the States, where there is obviously a niche market among baby Goths. But eventually she met her nemesis. One day her husband took the baby out in his cute little black Babygro with a sweet skull-and-crossbones motif, and people looked at him with the pram and smiled. Then they looked in the pram, and ran away.

'He looks like an Addams Family baby,' Tania admitted. 'So, for my son's social skills, I've had to change a little bit. He's gone to the cute end now – he has hand-made clothes and little fleecy bright colours, and it's all very cutesy. It's still not pastel, I might add.'

In case any of you are wondering if Tania inflicts her

unique brand of style only on other people and the inanimate, fear not. Among her colourful wardrobe is a trapeze artist's outfit from the Millennium Dome. It's yellow, pink and red, and wonderfully textured – just so you can try to visualize it. Quite why anyone would own, let alone wear, a Millennium Dome trapeze artist's costume is the sort of question that at the beginning of this piece one might reasonably have asked. Now it just seems churlish.

But even Tania hasn't worn it to the shops yet. Probably to help her son's social skills. However, she is thinking about it . . .

6

Secret Lives

�֍

'One man in his time plays many parts.' So says Jaques in
As You Like It, *and it is certainly true of the contributors to
this chapter – some furtive, some quietly heroic, others
rather colourful . . .*

*Marina Pepper stood for Parliament in the 2005 general
election. But before that – and when – she appeared on*
Home Truths *she had recently been appointed mayor of
Telscombe, a village near Brighton. Difficult to avoid the
obvious question then – and, no, it wasn't about what a
mayor actually does.*

The Page-Three Mayor
Marina Pepper, 2004

'Hmm.'

Those were Marina's exact words. Perhaps age had made
her coy.

'Oh no. I just used to do underwear modelling – any sort of
modelling I could get, really.'

Marina had started modelling at seventeen, a fact – unsurprisingly – she kept from her mother for as long as possible.
That, however, wasn't very long at all, because at eighteen she
became a *Playboy* Playmate.

'It was pretty fascinating,' Marina said, 'because I obviously got to go and stay with Hugh Hefner at the Playboy Mansion – in a rather quiet period, unfortunately. It was the eighties, and there was no Viagra, and he wasn't really partying. The strange thing is', she continued, '*Playboy*'s very, very straight. They would like their Playmates to be virgins if possible. Like the girls have to have bikini marks – the idea being this is the first time their nipples, or whatever, have ever seen the light of day. You were expected to be like a nun in your behaviour.'

Which is not, let's face it, what you might have expected.

'I was quite disappointed, I have to say,' Marina added.

Because she was – how should we put this? – looking forward to . . .

'Debauchery . . .'

That would be it.

'. . . in the Playboy Mansion, yes.'

After all, it's not as if the place wasn't designed for debauchery. Marina described walking into rooms and suddenly feeling the carpet bounce, and realizing the floor was one huge bed. And there'd be a mirror on the ceiling. And a jacuzzi so deep you could stand up in it with water bubbling right up to your neck, while a butler brought you drinks, and . . .

Anyway, Marina visited twice, and became Miss March in 1987. California and the good life beckoned. But Marina turned her back on it and came home.

'Well, I don't drive,' she explained, 'so Los Angeles isn't the place to be. And it really is about as shallow as they say, and it wasn't for me. I came back to England, gave it all up, and became a waitress. I thought, "Waitressing – very down to earth, meet people, be completely yourself, be judged on your ability to serve coffee, good honest work."'

If modelling was a long way from politics, waitressing was possibly further. Marina gave that job up to go travelling, ending up in Ireland – where she lived for three years creating a sustainable lifestyle, before it became fashionable. She ran a camp site in the summer, and made goat's cheese, campaigned against chemical factories, and organized recycling on the island she lived on. And then everything changed.

'Within weeks my boyfriend drowned and my stepfather – he'd been my father for most of my life – died. He was crushed at sea. And I realized I was sort of coming up to my mid-twenties. I really think that's an age where you've never really been touched by death, apart from the odd hamster. It was interesting to have to cope with mortality.

'I mean, I've coped with it in much bigger ways since. I've nursed a friend with cancer, that sort of thing. But it was a real "What am I going to do?" moment. If I died, what had I achieved? So I came back to England and did a journalism degree.'

Marina had been politically active since she was eighteen. The year that she appeared in *Playboy*, 1987, was also an election year, which probably makes her the only Playmate to also be a canvasser.

'I was stuffing envelopes and delivering leaflets for the Liberal Democrats because I sort of like it, in that sort of Tom Paine dissemination-of-information, promoting-democracy-at-grass-roots-level way. All through my life, whenever I've been in England during a general election, I've always gone along and helped in any way I can.'

When Marina had her children she thought about moving back to Ireland, or maybe to Spain. But political activism had obviously taken hold of her imagination.

'I decided there were things I could do in my own local community, and a couple of local councillors were going, "Why don't you stand?" And I just thought, "There's no way somebody like me can be a town councillor or a district councillor." And then, as soon as the election period was upon us, I went for it. I was determined to win – and I did.' Marina chuckled at the memory.

And, amazingly perhaps, the opposition didn't bring up her modelling career in an attempt to besmirch her profile with the voters. They might have missed a trick, but now she'll be judged on her record in office rather than on a bunch of photographs taken back in 1987. Anyway, as Marina revealed, the cat's out the bag now.

'I was in the pub the other night, and these lads, who are normally quite noisy and boisterous, were absolutely silent. And I sort of turned round and said, "Are you guys all right?" And then one of them just looked at the floor and went, "We're shy."'

However, Marina isn't just a councillor: she's the mayor. Not a mayoress but the mayor. Officially her husband is the consort, but everyone – confusingly perhaps – calls him the mayoress. And her children, Boudicca and Charlie, are the mayorlets – which you might think is exciting enough, but this also means they get to go free on the bouncy castles at the region's fairs. This is a good thing, because the children have a very developed bouncy-castle habit – not quite a dependency, you understand – and Marina was struggling to maintain it, especially as the opportunity for them to go on bouncy castles has increased so markedly now she has to go and open the fairs and announce the raffle and tombola winners.

Marina, unlike mayors in all those old black-and-white public-information films, doesn't walk around in a gown with a fur collar and a chain of office. She does, however, host parties, open the aforementioned fairs, and network. And, if all of that sounds a bit tepid for someone who started a recycling programme in the 1980s and was once the apple of many a teenager's eye, then fear not. Marina brings her own sensibility to the politics.

'I do actually really like the politics, and sort of uniting groups of people. And even if they traditionally come from opposing points of view let's find some common ground. And also when the public come to the meetings I like stopping the meeting to explain to them what is going on, because I really want to make the local-government meetings so interesting that the public actually want to come. There was a meeting last night and they were complaining that they weren't allowed to ask questions once a meeting was under way. And I was going, "No, you can't. But no one's stopping you from heckling. You can say what you like, and it's up to us how we respond." And I think that's exciting, and that's how it should be.'

It doesn't take much to imagine that Marina Pepper isn't your typical mayor, and that her power-to-the-people stance is not necessarily warmly embraced by her fellow councillors.

'It is a departure. I believe the Madame Clerk said the dignity of the office was temporarily suspended.' But 'I do take the role seriously. Whether I'd want to go all the way to Parliament . . . I'm developing an interest in that. It's so fundamental that we get my generation – I mean I'm thirty-six – interested in politics.'

Marina's life now is a long way away from that bouncy floor in the Playboy Mansion. And she has absolutely no regrets.

'I don't think I was a great model anyway. I mean, I think if I hadn't gone into politics and become a mayor I don't think my pictures would have ever seen the light of day.'

In case you were wondering, Marina was finally tempted to stand for Parliament in the 2005 general election. Her *Playboy* spread didn't become the headline, but she didn't win either.

Stephen Waldron is the son of Malcolm Waldron, once the head of the plutonium section at Harwell, later dean of the Faculty of Metallurgy and Materials Technology at Surrey University, where they've just named a laboratory after him. Now everyone knows what his father did, but it wasn't always that way.

Due to the officially secret nature of all things Harwellian, Malcolm Waldron could never discuss what he did with his wife and growing family. When Stephen did eventually realize the scope of his father's work he was gobsmacked and impressed, and perhaps a little shocked. After all by this time it was 1970, he was fifteen and he had assumed long ago that he knew everything worth knowing about his parents. Wrong!

My Dad the Nuclear Scientist
Stephen Waldron, 2005

The story that still takes Stephen's breath away concerns his father's role in exporting the first bit of plutonium from Britain to France, our ally.

'So he was responsible for taking I think it was one or two kilograms of plutonium,' Stephen remembers, 'which must be worth millions and millions of pounds today, to General de Gaulle. When he got to whichever airport it was in Paris, they had this massive cavalcade. He said eight motorbike outriders and about six cars went down the Champs-Elysées and crossed over on to Ile de la Cité to the atomic energy centre – and all of it filmed for television. General de Gaulle shook my father's hand, took the case, and put it in this huge safe.'

And if all that doesn't sound extraordinary enough, just wait till you hear what happened to the plutonium next.

'The next day my father went in with his opposite number from the French programme. They took the case out of the safe, slung it on the back seat of their Deux Chevaux or whatever it was, and drove off thirty-five miles south of Paris to the laboratories with no escort or anything, just on the back seat – literally. My father said it was just literally on the back seat of the car, and it actually fell off once or twice into the well of the car.'

A pretty blasé, naive sort of approach to things from today's standpoint.

Stephen and his family lived on the Harwell estate in Abingdon. Their neighbours were other Harwell families, and while the estate was open to the public, no one other than the milkman ventured in. Stephen was aware of growing up in an unusual environment – different and special in a way he couldn't understand. The children of the Harwell scientists were all uncommonly bright – exam pass levels were always 100 per cent. And this sense of strangeness was only exacerbated by Harwell itself.

'It seemed like a strange almost semi-fictional place, because we were never allowed in. And my mother hated it, because in the whole time from 1949 to . . . well, she got married in '52, so '52 to '66 – when my father left – there was only one social event the wives ever went to. Can you imagine that in a work environment? So even my mother was never allowed to talk to my father about work.'

Stephen's sense of isolation and oddness was compounded by his family's faith. They belonged to the Plymouth Brethren, one of the most closed sects in the world. Consequently, the children couldn't have any friends outside of their Church, and couldn't watch TV, listen to the radio or read the newspapers. And cinema was completely forbidden.

Then the Brethren cast the Waldrons out. Stephen's father had stood up to some of the Church's practices and behaviour, and so that was that. It meant they could have no contact with relatives or friends who remained within the Brethren. It meant watching your family walk away from you, and deliberately not talking to you – experiences that must have been bewildering and painful for children.

When Stephen was eleven the Waldrons left Harwell and moved to Guildford, and, with the links to the Brethren properly severed, life took on a very different complexion.

'We actually began to explore beyond the edges of ex-Exclusive Brethren and began to realize that the world was full of . . . I think it was like "Oh my goodness, it's a multicoloured world out there and there's some amazing people."'

And the life of a dean of faculty was very different from that of a secret government scientist. Still, given his father's job and religious background, it must have surprised Stephen when his father sat down and opened up about his previous work.

'We're a very, very close family, and our world was opening up at a phenomenal rate. So we'd gone from this Plymouth Brethren world, which is incredibly tight – it's difficult to explain in a few minutes, but very tight – to my mother's dream, which was to be the wife of the dean of faculty in Surrey University: very expansive, with masses of socializing and entertaining. We had people back all the time.

'We were incredibly precocious children, because my father was introducing us to a very exciting world because he got involved in things like the silver content of Roman coins. That was one of the research projects: showing that you could tell the Roman Empire crashed, because the Roman coins had dropped in silver – the silver value.'

Malcolm Waldron also designed the first artificial hip joints – an achievement which resulted in his picture appearing on the first, coloured, chequebooks that came out with pictures on. 'And so as kids you'd think, "Oh my goodness, my father's quite interesting after all," you know?'

When Malcolm wasn't inventing artificial hips or measuring the decline of the Roman Empire by the drop in the silver content of its coinage he was a very dedicated family man: gardening, making and repairing things, introducing the kids to exotic foreign foods, and dragging them around rock pools on holiday to collect winkles and mussels. All the while puffing and blowing – which would embarrass the children, who thought their dad was just a very ordinary sort of man. Until they started hearing his stories –

'Stories about accidents where people may even have died – or not died immediately, died over a period of time,' Stephen remembers. 'Stories which were slightly scary, to do with spies at Harwell, contact with spies, and people being discovered. A typical one would be about Klaus Fuchs. Klaus Fuchs was a notorious spy, who had worked with America through the Second World War developing the atomic bomb. And then after the war he came and worked in Harwell – but not in my father's department. And the Americans were not being very helpful to Britain or any of the Allies about plutonium, because of course the bomb was built of plutonium. My father was on the peaceful side, trying to build a nuclear reactor for power – the fast-breeder reactor at Dounreay. And they were all looking for a stable form of plutonium, and they knew they had to combine it with something – some other elements – to get it in a stable state.

'The story, as he told it, has Klaus Fuchs one day bump into my father and give him a slip of paper – I think literally my father said the back of an envelope – on which were some scribbled numbers. And he muttered to my father, "Well, Malcolm, I know this is the key to understanding the nature of plutonium that can be used for peaceful purposes. I noticed these numbers when I wasn't meant to in Los Alamos" – which is the American centre for nuclear research – "and I think this will be helpful." And then he shuffled off, and my father never spoke to him again. And of course he was arrested soon after and bunged in prison for nine years. So there was no interaction, just this piece of paper. And this was like a grid reference. I mean, I'm not a scientist – I'm an architect – but a grid reference of numbers was the key to this particular arrangement or lattice, I think, was the word he used. And over the next years it proved that this was in fact the key bit of information. I don't think anybody knows that story, because only my father knew it, and I think if he'd told the story at the time he might have got into trouble.'

Malcolm, perhaps unsurprisingly, died of leukaemia. But neither Stephen nor his father were bitter over this legacy from Harwell.

'We talked about it when he was dying, because he took a long time to die, and he just said, "Well, it's part of the territory." Nobody really knew how dangerous it was, nobody understood it, and there's no bitterness in the family at all about it. We shrug our shoulders and think that's part of the rich tapestry of life, I suppose.'

Nonetheless, there is a startling contrast between a man who was a regular dad, huffing and puffing, winkling and gardening, and a man who kept extraordinary secrets for so much of his life, and of necessity had to exclude his family from his working life.

'And for my mother, when we talk together about these things, it's just a huge hole where she knows almost nothing at all. And in fact it frustrates her. So I think just at that level you know you spend your time thinking, "I wonder what really went on? I wonder if my father was lonely? I wonder what pressures he was under? I wonder whether it was hard to carry his secrets?" And you wonder how many other things went on that perhaps he couldn't tell us about?'

*Secrets of a different magnitude now – but equally
surprising in their own way. When Sharon Cannon's father,
an international businessman, died, she and her two sisters
heard about it only through television news coverage. Sharon
was vaguely aware of her father's complex life, but it was his
death that revealed the tangled marital web he'd spun over
the years . . .*

Dad's Other Wives
Sharon Cannon, 2001

'My mother, Marion, was the first wife,' Sharon explains. 'My
father then went on to marry three times more. Each wife had
the same initial. The second wife was German, the third
Swiss, and the fourth wife Polish.'

When Sharon was seven years old, her father, whose work as
a civil engineer took him across Europe, left her mother. Sharon
didn't see him again for seventeen years. It was Sharon's grandmother – her father's mother – who kept in touch with Sharon's
mother and the children. In fact, in a curious set-up, Sharon's
grandmother was in touch with all four wives.

'She was the overseer of arrangements,' says Sharon. 'We
couldn't visit her without an appointment, in case we bumped
into anybody. When we visited her, she always had the right
photographs up of each family – right down to the children's
drawings on the fridge! We adored her, although once she got
my mother's name mixed up with another wife's name.'

At first, each of the wives had no knowledge of the previous
wives. But over time they gradually became aware of each other.

'My father's last wife, the Polish wife,' explains Sharon,
'told us that she'd been married to my dad for some time
when she found out about the previous wife, and a little later
about the one before that. Then, clearing out some papers,
she found a photo of myself and my young son. "What's this?"

she demanded. "Another wife?" He replied, "No. That's my daughter and my grandson."'

Sharon's father died in an unfortunate accident, hanging lights from the balcony at his mother's home. He slipped and fell, and died of a brain haemorrhage. He was only fifty-nine.

The funeral, inevitably, was very confusing.

'Nobody knew who anyone was!' says Sharon. 'There was much speculation – "Could she be a wife? She looks the type." His fourth wife came over and asked, "How many of your father's wives have you met?" The whole thing was like an Ayckbourn play!'

Although bizarre, it was also painful. In the eulogies, her father was revealed as a man whom Sharon knew nothing about – an opera fan, someone involved in conservation, a man who loved architecture.

When Sharon's grandmother died, she left her granddaughter a trunk of photographs. Among them were sets of pictures of each family (the second wife had had three children with Sharon's father) and each wife. The funeral might have revealed the depth of her father's personality, and the breath of his interests and passions, for the first time, but the trunk gave Sharon an introduction to an extended family she never knew she had. The photos also brought to life a man who had kept so much silent and closed away, who had allowed his daughter to see so little of his true self. It was, Sharon says, exciting, disturbing and cathartic in equal measure.

From the clandestine life of a father to the secret lives of toothbrushes now.

In the reckless spirit that so defined Home Truths, *the programme urged listeners to unburden their consciences after Chris Brooks did just that and told how he had used his sister-in-law's toothbrush to clean his dog's teeth. Chris's misdeeds were born of the delicious innocence of youth. But Barbara Boyce's, which also involve toothbrushes, came from an altogether darker place.*

Unusual Uses for Toothbrushes
Barbara Boyce, 2003

'I used to have a Labrador who had the dog breath problem, and I'd read somewhere that using smoker's tooth powder was a good remedy for this. My husband of the time – who soon became ex, because of his desperate love for the stuff in brown bottles – used to use this preparation, so the obvious thing to do was to use his tooth powder on the dog, who did have her own toothbrush, at first. However, as my spouse's behaviour became more and more obnoxious, there were times when his toothbrush was used on the long-suffering Labrador. He always suspected, but was never quite sure.

I'm sure that many women are familiar with the feeling of getting small acts of revenge against erring partners, but where did I get the idea? My mother, the essence of prim-and-properness, once admitted to me that she was so sick of my father peeing on the toilet seat – not even lifting it up, never mind putting it down – that she'd started wiping it up with his face flannel.'

Hannah Finch also has a toothbrush-related confession.

'Apparently, when I was no more than three or four, my mother came upstairs to find me dutifully helping out with her housework. I was cleaning the loo. With a toothbrush. As she stood transfixed with terror, little angel that I was, and still am, I turned round and said, 'Don't worry, it's Daddy's' – leaving my poor mother to wonder how many times I'd helped out in this way before.'

Yuli Somme's dad, Sven, was a proper no-bones-about-it hero. During the Second World War he worked for the Norwegian resistance, first publishing a forbidden newspaper, then, in a more active capacity, photographing German military installations. He was captured, but on his way to interrogation, torture and the firing squad he made the kind of audacious escape you wouldn't believe if you saw it in a film. This was followed by an epic eight-week journey, during which he was chased by nine hundred Nazis over unforgiving mountains until he reached Sweden. He died in 1961, when Yuli was just five years old, but left good records of his deeds.

In 2004 Yuli and her sister retraced his epic journey and told us how Sven first got away from the Nazis.

My Father – the Hero
Yuli Somme, 2004

'He was handcuffed to a Hungarian soldier, and they were on a boat going across the Molde Fjord and anchored at a place called Åndalsnes for the night, ready to take a train up to Dombås the next day. He was told that he would be interrogated and shot. During the night the soldier, who had been on duty for thirty-six hours and was very, very tired, offered to unhandcuff my father, so that they could both lie down and have a sleep.'

This proved to be a fatal mistake for the Hungarian guard, who was shot as a result. Meanwhile, Sven Somme was escaping into the mountains.

'He knew the mountains very well,' Yuli explains, 'because his work took him into the lakes in the mountains – he was a marine biologist. If you worked in intelligence you would always have an escape route planned, so he'd already planned his route across to Sweden.'

Nonetheless, whether you knew it or not, the terrain was extremely hazardous. Sven had to climb and walk some two hundred miles. Despite it being June, there was still a lot of snow on the peaks and the weather was very wet and cold, making the steep ascents and descents highly dangerous. And all the time he knew the Germans would be hunting for him. The year before his brother had been caught, tortured and shot after a major attack on the Germans.

'So once they linked up the names Papa knew that he would have been shot. They sent nine hundred soldiers after him, and even a week after his escape he encountered some in the mountains. Obviously he managed to hide.'

Sven was so afraid of capture by the Germans that he even hid from his own fellow Norwegians – a practice that endangered his health, as he had no easy access to food and water. In fact, in order to help him, the first group of people who encountered him had to go to unlikely extremes, as Yuli explains.

'The first lot of people actually captured him, because he was very scared and didn't want to meet anybody. They'd heard that he'd escaped, and they really wanted to help him – a young group of people. They went out and found him, and then hid him for about a week in a little barn and fed him.'

Eventually Sven reached Sweden, emotionally and physically exhausted. From there he found his way to England.

Like so many combatants from the war, he rarely talked about what he had done, and as he died when Yuli was just five her memories of him are understandably few and hazy. She certainly never had time to talk to him about his wartime experiences. However, he did write a lot of them down, and Yuli's mother turned his descriptions into a book about ten years ago. The book inspired Yuli to follow in her father's footsteps – across that hazardous mountain terrain.

'It was Ellie, my sister, who for years and years had suggested that we follow this route and try and contact some of the people who had helped him. And then a Norwegian cousin said to us, "You do realize it's the sixtieth anniversary next year, and that might be a good time to do it?"'

So the sisters decided to make their pilgrimage, Yuli expecting little more than a hearty trek through the mountains with her rucksack.

Very quickly, she started to recognize the places he had described in his book. 'He put down quite extensive detail of the route and features along the way. And it was quite exciting for us when we were planning the walk to actually see these features on the map. And then as we walked the route there was a certain forest at a certain corner of the lake that he'd got lost in, and there we were trying to find the same track.'

Following in Sven's footsteps encouraged the sisters to try to imagine what it must have been like for their father as he fled the Nazis.

'Well, for him there was a mixture of terror, exhaustion, emotional exhaustion and then elation and excitement,' Yuli says. 'And all sorts of things went through his mind at the time; and all of these emotions he wrote in this book – which we would read to each other at night while we were camping, and we would try to recapture what it might have felt like. I think for many post-war children like us it's quite interesting, as you get older, to try and imagine what it might have been like for those wartime people.'

Yuli and her sister, as part of the generations born after the war, could only guess what it must have been like to face what Sven faced. However, the trip helped them to understand – not least because of all the people they met who, to the sisters' surprise, had known and remembered him.

'Well, that was really a revelation to us. When we got to Molde, which was where we lived as children and where this expedition started, we were met by a whole deputation of people. And we met his old housekeeper; we met three of the people who had been directly involved in helping him through the mountains, feeding him and clothing him.'

And these people told stories that brought their father back to life. Despite the passing of the years, they still remembered him – a revealing testament to the kind of man Sven Somme was. And the stories have travelled the generations, so now the children of the people that knew him know about Sven too.

His housekeeper remembered his great sense of humour, despite the unbelievable stress he was under. The school he worked in was occupied by the Germans, who would be sitting upstairs while he was in the basement producing his resistance newspapers.

'He had a lot of cheek,' Yuli observes with some understatement. 'You know, the way he escaped was just pure cheek – walking straight past a group of Nazi soldiers as if he was going for a little walk, a little stroll, and then once he got round the corner he belted along.'

The townsfolk presented Yuli with a package containing the shoes Sven had worn when he was crossing the mountains. A woman had kept them for sixty years – saving them from her burning house when it caught fire. One can only imagine how important they were to her if she was prepared to take such a risk for a pair of old shoes.

'They're flat, boring, brown wartime shoes. They're just worn out – the bottoms would have been hopeless in mountains. Very scuffed – you can still see the shape of his feet.'

And Yuli has retraced the path they followed. She and her sister read and reread Sven's account avidly on their trip, and as they went – as they felt the rocks under their feet and heard the tales from those who knew and cherished him – the story grew. At the end she'd discovered that her father was a hero to many, but had also become much more of a father to her.

'I feel that I got to know him a lot more through hearing the stories, reading the book over and over again, and trying to go through the emotions that he went through. And I do feel so much closer to him.'

Sven Somme – hero.

Until now, Owen O'Mahoney's contribution to the comfort of Britain's male population has gone unnoticed and unheralded. For two years, Owen – on Her Majesty's service – selflessly carried out extensive high-altitude testing of those intimate garments charged with holding male reproductive equipment in place. Or, to put it another way, Owen was an underpants test pilot for Marks & Spencer. Which, when you think about it, doesn't make much sense either. Perhaps we should let him explain . . .

Underpants Test Pilot
Owen O'Mahoney, 2000

Owen was brought up in comparatively poor circumstances in Ireland in which shoes were a luxury and underpants optional. For financial reasons probably, his mother didn't take up this option, and it was only when Owen joined the RAF that he discovered that he had been lagging behind the rest of the population.

'We were all issued with four pairs of enormous knee-length Aertex bloomers, with a vertical slot at the front. I assume it was at the front, because it was on the opposite side to a label bearing a large arrow signifying that they were government property and bearing a ten-digit part number to ensure that they could never be confused with other military hardware,' Owen tells us.

Owen wore these underpants with pride for a number of years, alarmingly. 'My wife even patched them when the small Aertex holes developed into anything larger. But in 1967 I became aware from the various macho advertisements that this type of underwear was passé and that, if one was to succeed in life, then it could only be done with the new Y-fronts, which, in a word, stopped things hanging about.'

Owen was not one to be suckered by hype, so he ignored these claims from the manufacturers for many a year. And his wife kept darning. 'I did however ensure that my successful "macho" mates never saw me in my voluminous "shreddies",' he admits.

However, he was about to come a cropper in the most unexpected fashion – through ultra-violet lighting, which was introduced into nightclubs and dance halls so that the more eagle-eyed patrons could cop a view of the underwear of women caught in the lighting.

'One particular night I went to a club in Germany. I was wearing my dark-blue Burton's "Director" suit, with only four payments to make before it was mine. I sat down to rest after a particularly vigorous dash around the dance floor to the strains of Glenn Miller's "American Patrol". Olga, an Amazonian Russian woman, had asked me to dance, and from what I understood had said something about being a trumpeter with the Bolshoi Ballet.

'Now I can understand Olga wanting to dance with me – I was, after all, tall, distinguished, fair haired and, according to my mother and all her friends, handsome. Nonetheless, I was a little puzzled why a Russian lady, who couldn't speak much English, had chosen me for the ladies' invitation dance. It was only when I sat down panting and unravelling my ribs, temporarily damaged by the ample Olga, that I noticed that the UV lighting was highlighting the now luminous seams of my underpants. Shock! Horror! I was the only one with seams below my knees. It must have been obvious to the aforementioned lady that I was wearing Government Issue! I skulked around the edge of the dance floor away from the humiliating lights and caught the bus home. With the benefit of experience and hindsight, it is now plain to me that Olga was a KGB spy trying to find out the, probably classified, part number on my underpants.'

In the interests of national security, and so we could all sleep safely in our beds, Owen finally succumbed to the manufacturer's hype and his wife dashed off to M & S to buy him some plain white combed-cotton Y-fronts.

'These new underpants gave me the courage and confidence to face the world. Everything was neatly packaged, and as a result – if the manufacturers were to be believed – I was now about to reap the benefits.'

Owen began to notice a curious correlation between the wearing of his new underpants and a string of good fortune that saw his career flourish.

'I started off with six pairs and began to prosper. Promoted to sergeant, commissioned, trained as a pilot, posted to Singapore – it was all happening just like the manufacturers said. By the time that I got back to the UK, some three years later, it was time to invest in a further two pairs, but to my chagrin they had changed the style – higher on the leg, and with less equipment storage space.'

Owen tried them for a while, but he wasn't happy and, understandably enough, feared that the vertical trajectory of his career (no pun intended) might lose momentum. It was time, he decided, to put pen to paper.

Marks & Spencer Ltd

Dear Sirs

I have for some time now been an ardent collector of your white combed-cotton 'Y' fronted underpants size 34″–36″. My wife recently bought me two pairs and I regret to inform you that they are far from satisfactory. I notice that the overlap at the front on the newer versions has been reduced (a saving of material perhaps?). Now I am a man of modest proportions, but the upshot is that things keep dropping out.

I am, for my sins, a flying instructor in Her Majesty's Royal Air Force and when strapped into my aircraft, upside down at 18,000 feet, this is uncomfortable. Not to mention that when I apply 'g' forces the said overlap becomes an effective tourniquet!

I would ask you to reconsider the design of these underpants, otherwise I shall be forced to place my annual order for four pairs elsewhere.

Yours sincerely, etc.

One can easily imagine the consternation this daunting threat caused – perhaps an emergency board meeting. Then came the reply:

Dear Flight Lieutenant O'Mahoney

Thank you for your letter. We are sorry that you are unhappy about your recent purchase; however, you will be pleased to know that we are in the process of redesigning this particular style.

Please find enclosed two pairs of the new prototypes with our compliments and we would appreciate your comments after you have tested them in the unusual conditions in which you work.

Yours sincerely
F. A. L. Cook (ex Flt Lt Navigator)

'This continued for about two years,' Owen explains. 'New prototypes arrived, I would whizz them up to 20,000 feet, do a few loops in them, roll them, spin them, and finish with a stall turn before sitting down to writing an in-depth report covering such aspects as security, accessibility, comfort and suitability for astronauts. I assume that the manufacturers had already carried out the more basic tests on the elastic, washability, shrinkage etc.'

The high-altitude test programme was paid for by Her Majesty, who kindly provided the aircraft and the fuel. Everybody was happy: Owen got free underpants, and M & S got in-depth reports. He even suggested that coloured versions might catch on.

So next time you're buying some new underpants – especially if they're not white – why not doff your cap or offer up a quiet salute to Owen O'Mahoney, who did his duty for Queen, country and male comfort.

But for her brother, what might Linda Layton's life have turned out like? Whatever the answer, it probably wouldn't have included impressing her son in such a monumental way . . .

Brush With the Famous
Linda Layton, 2001

'The year was 1965. I was fifteen, and invited to my first twenty-first birthday extravaganza in a grand house in Benhall,' Linda remembers. 'I fell in love at first sight with the singer of the group Jokers Wild, and it seemed mutual – he kept his eyes on me all the time he was singing, and during the break when the disco took over he came and danced with me without saying a word – very cool!

Eventually we got to names. His was David. He asked to take me home when the do was over. I said yes immediately, but my brother stepped in and warned him I was only fifteen. Thanks a lot! I was broken-hearted, though he gave me a passionate goodbye kiss.'

Linda thought of the singer often without ever seeing him again, until one night at her son's arty school in Hampshire. Like her he was in the library, waiting to talk to the maths teacher.

'I hid behind a pillar, and when my son asked what I was doing I told him I had spotted an old flame. He checked out the man in question and said, "Mum, that's David Gilmour – you know, Pink Floyd?" I was deeply embarrassed, and gave the maths teacher a miss – though I think I went up in my son's estimation!

'Two weeks ago I met the birthday girl – who told me she had bumped into him again last summer and all he could remember of her twenty-first was a beautiful girl called Linda!'

Aaah – probably best kept as a happy memory!

Our next story also involves fighting in wars. But if Sven Somme was a hero who kept quiet because that was characteristic of his generation, Andy Hopwood did so because of his unease and shame at the morally murky action he was involved in – somewhere in Africa, though even now he won't say where. When he finally told his partner, Sharon, about his past she was truly startled. How did a seventeen-year-old British boy end up killing, and nearly getting himself killed, in the midst of a guerrilla war whose causes he knew nothing about?

Soldier, Fighter
Andy Hopwood, 2005

'I went with my ju-jitsu instructor to a seminar that was being put on by a military instruction team, and we did a whole day's training in their techniques,' Andy says, describing how he started on a career as a soldier of fortune. 'And it was really interesting. He explained that they were looking for people who they thought might like to go to their school – train within the school – and I jumped at the chance, even though I was only seventeen.'

The school was in Africa, but Andy wouldn't be specific as to where, for reasons that will become apparent. He went to a place on the South Atlantic coast for three months, and stayed five years. It was, as you might imagine, a complete culture shock for a seventeen-year-old.

'Immediately from the airport I was met by a very brusque man who shouted at me and beckoned me and pointed in the back of a truck. I jumped in the back, where I met Joe, who became a very close friend. Joe was from Stockholm, in Sweden. We didn't have any other greeting other than just pointing to our room, and he left us there for a few hours.'

Andy and Joe were in an army barracks. Yet they still believed that they were there only to improve their martial-arts skills. The possibility that they were there for something more serious hadn't dawned on them. But Andy was in for a rude awakening when he had his first training session.

'I had the worst beating I've ever had in my life,' Andy remembers. 'He beat me literally to a pulp. He didn't stop hitting me from the first strike – the guy literally just hit me until my bladder opened and my bowels opened. I was cut about the face and body. I was in tears. I'd gone from total arrogance and self-belief to a hospital bed.'

Despite this treatment, Andy was determined to stick it

out and was still convinced that he was there simply to become better at martial arts. The realization that he was in an army didn't come till later.

'That was some months later, because by then I'd gone through initial combat training and I thought, "Right, I'm going to stay here and learn as much as I can." But we hadn't been given any military training, there'd been no weapons involved, and no soldiering. But that followed on quickly, afterwards. And again it was presented as would you like to do this, would you like to do that.'

As if he had a choice. And then they went out on a military expedition.

'Yeah, the barracks that we were at was attacked. There was a lot of guerrilla warfare going on within the country, and the base was attacked. There was some mortar fire. I was in bed asleep, quickly threw on some clothes, and ran out to find out what was happening.'

Andy ran out into the parade ground. By now he was armed, and he found himself involved in quite a skirmish and face to face with the realization that he could be killed and might have to kill.

'Yeah, yeah, yeah – it was the first moment. I mean, in those situations you're never sure you've actually killed somebody, but something inside knows. Getting back after the whole situation had calmed down, having some time, there's a lot of torment goes on in those situations.'

For a seventeen-year-old this must have been a shocking and traumatic experience. And yet Andy didn't question why he was there or who he was with, even though he knew he wasn't fighting under the British flag.

'No, not at the time. There was no question of being a mercenary, because I was literally a guest in the situation. There was no payment – it was just bed, board and I was doing it out of duty to my friends at the time. And I was a kid, I was excited, it was exhilarating. I was always terrified, but there was always an adrenalin rush as well.'

His experiences only got worse. Andy witnessed some horrendous scenes, and at one point was caught up in an attack by a suicide bomber.

'More than one, but yeah,' Andy says, correcting any false impressions we might have about how dangerous his life had become. 'One morning I was in my room, in the shower, and the whole place shook. A vehicle had been driven in packed with explosives – in through the main gates, at the time the guard watch was changing, and the civilians were all coming in to start their day's work. I arrived in the main courtyard to find the walls of the offices literally split apart, lots of injuries. There were middle-aged ladies lying there with literally limbs missing, soldiers that I knew with shards of glass embedded in their bodies. We had to cope with that, and we treated the injured as best we could. I was out there for just under five years, and I guess four years of that was in a military situation, I suppose.'

Many of Andy's friends were killed in action. Joe the Swede – his closest friend – was shot by a sniper in the capital city when the two of them went shopping there on a day off.

'I guess that was the catalyst – Joe's death was a catalyst for me to start thinking about all the other close friends that I'd lost,' Andy says. 'So I struggled on for a few months, but made a decision that "That's it, I'm leaving." And I came back. My parents, every time I'd been home, had their way of coping with it, which I suppose is a very British way of coping with it, which was to pretend it hadn't happened, pretend it wasn't happening. And I was broken – completely mentally and emotionally broken – by the time I came back. So my thought process was "Well, if that's how my family's coping with it, that's how I deal with it." So I shut it out.'

Andy got a job at the Longbridge plant on the production

line, and never talked about his experiences until one night in Newquay when he revealed everything to Sharon. His love for her and the peace he found in the life they shared together made him feel able to unburden himself. According to Sharon, Andy wrote down all his experiences – an exercise that can often help make sense of everything you're feeling.

'It seemed the right way for me to banish the demons, I suppose – to write it down. It just seemed the right thing to do.'

Somehow, writing everything down took the experiences and memories that were trapped in Andy's head and made them less personal. They'd been trapped inside him, and now he was able to look down at them on a piece of paper. Still, what Andy had seen and done in those momentous, formative years took their toll.

'I guess I went out thinking I was indestructible, and I came back, as I say, mentally and emotionally completely gone. And every time I hear a news story or see a news story about any kind of military exercise it really saddens me. The whole thing has made me appreciate that it doesn't matter who you are, you should aim to live in peace.'

Ray Bowler felt that he'd been missing out all his life – on women's clothing. So, to right this wrong, some years ago he tried on a few garments more traditionally associated with the female form . . .

I Feel Gorgeous!
Ray Bowler, 2001

'Apart from the nice little diamanté earring, I'd pass for a bloke in the street,' Ray begins. His interest in women's clothing started in his twenties. 'Blokes' clothes are fairly dull. There's some lovely, sensuous fabrics in women's clothing.

They hang off your body in a different way. They are rather delicious . . .'

He remembers when he first tried on women's attire: 'Years ago – I was married at the time – there was one dress of my wife's I liked a great deal, and I did wear that on occasion.'

One part of Ray responded with 'Oh! At last!' and the other part sternly told him, 'You shouldn't be doing this! This isn't what men do!' The dress in question was a black, sensual chiffony affair – 'all the fabrics that are out of bounds for blokes. And I thought, "I feel gorgeous!"'

Ray's friends suddenly saw a different man – in more ways than one. 'I could tell by their faces – they were delighted! It was great!'

He's gone on to develop his own way of dressing: not so much dressing as a woman, just dressing as Ray. As David Bowie once said when pulled up for wearing women's clothes, 'They're my clothes.'

'I'm trying to take this away from the erotic tag it usually carries,' says Ray, 'I want other people out there to feel it's a legitimate part of their being, and not something preserved for the bedroom.'

Men, Ray thinks, don't love their bodies enough – unlike women – and his clothes preference is to do with thinking better of himself.

'Most of my friends are women – especially Di, who's gorgeous and immensely supportive. All I want really is "clothing rights", to show myself to be vulnerable at times and less aggressive as a bloke. If you wear something with shoulder straps, it feels enormously vulnerable.'

Ray's been to clubs for cross-dressers. 'It wasn't my world at all – it's all rather sad. I want to be honest about it. I want it to be part of life. I'm happy to be a bloke, but there's another side to me that wants to get out and flaunt itself.'

7

Love is a Many-Splendoured Thing . . .

❦

From couples declaring their love in the Arctic permafrost to romance in the Guatemalan rainforest, from couples who remarry – each other – to newly-weds whose love withstands everything, including the mother-in-law going on the honeymoon, Home Truths *has heard it all. Love may be a many-splendoured thing. It certainly is a very weird thing.*

A year on from her divorce, Anne Barbour decided to put painful memories behind her with the help of a cake, a mallet and a flock of seagulls . . .

Cake Wake
Anne Barbour, 2002

Divorce is awful, and Anne's was no different. During the upsetting process of clearing out cupboards and drawers, Anne came across a poignant reminder of that special day twenty-five years ago – the top layer of her wedding cake in more or less perfect condition.

Instead of dumping it in a bin bag, Anne decided then and there, 'I can't throw this away. I've got to use it in a very positive way!'

Friends said, 'Achieve closure! Throw it in the Thames!' But Anne wanted more. A party was the thing.

'I'll call it a "Cake Wake",' she thought, inviting a few close friends – 'mourners' she called them – to a ceremony in which the cake would symbolize the end of her marriage.

The evening, which would have been Anne's twenty-fifth wedding anniversary, went with a swing. Champagne flowed, fireworks exploded. 'The neighbours thought there was a firing squad in the garden,' Anne remembers. And a splendid dinner was had.

In the corner of the room, on an altar-like arrangement, the cake awaited its fate. Anne had replaced the traditional model of bride and groom with a big gold candle in the shape of a pig. 'It was a cake shrine, and attached to it was a plaque which read, "In Memoriam 1976–2001".'

The time came to 'cut' the cake. But, in place of a knife, Anne wielded a wooden meat mallet, adorned with a red ribbon, which one of her friends had had the foresight to bring along as a sort of replacement for the traditional horseshoe given to the bride. 'I was told to bash the cake up! Everyone felt it would be very therapeutic.' So the cake received a good walloping, but it remained stubbornly cake-ish in shape.

As the wine flowed again, the party forgot about the remains in the corner. The next day, however, Anne's friends rang to say they were concerned that the cake was still there. Anne, resourceful to the last, told them not to worry. She had a plan.

That weekend, while visiting Southampton, Anne took the cake down to the waterfront and placed it on a wooden pile sticking up out of the water. What happened next was reminiscent of a scene from Hitchcock's film *The Birds*.

'Within minutes seagulls came from every direction and devoured the cake. It was gone! With the sun just setting, it was wonderful – and a very dramatic end to the ceremony.'

Turning back to her car, Anne saw what appeared to be a final comment on the state of her marriage.

'It was plastered with bird droppings! I just laughed and laughed. To me they were strokes of good luck. There is life after divorce.'

When Clive and Heidi and two friends went to the South Wales coast for a short holiday, Clive planned to pop the question, quietly hoping he'd sweep Heidi off her feet, metaphorically speaking . . .

A Muddy Proposal
Heidi Collier and Clive Dowling, 2003

Clive and Heidi and two friends were in Saundersfoot in South Wales. It was about 8 p.m., and as the other two enjoyed a walk down to the harbour Heidi and Clive sat on the sea wall, a passer-by took their photos, and Clive proposed.

As they stood, caught up in the excitement, Clive lifted Heidi off the ground and swung her around in the air. But before they could stop they both toppled over the wall. The tide was out and the drop was over twenty feet, but fortunately their fall was broken by the oily and muddy sludge the sea left behind. They landed side by side, to have and to hold, in sickness and in health . . .

'Are you alive, love?' Clive asked.

Luckily she was.

'Have I still got the ring on?' were Heidi's first words.

There was, understandably, quite a bit of commotion, with ambulances and the coastguard. Even a helicopter was called. And of course there was the requisite large audience on the pier – Saundersfoot had probably never seen the like before.

Heidi and Clive managed to get themselves out of the harbour, got checked over by the ambulance crew, and then had

to walk back to their hotel stinking, covered in mud and oil –
the laughing stock of the village.

Thankfully, Heidi is still planning to marry Clive, and the
best man's speech is already written . . .

*Mark and Nargess got married for the first time in 1971.
Nargess says that for her it was a case of love at first sight,
and they married soon after meeting. They'd been together
for some twelve years when Nargess's mother died, and
Mark says his wife became very withdrawn. For him this
was 'more a final straw on a rather doubtful contract'.*

Second Time Around
Mark and Nargess Stevens, 1998

Nargess says that at the time of their first marriage she was
rather young and immature, and didn't understand the
subtleties of the British character. She describes the Mark of
that time as a rather reserved, cold Englishman, and says they
clashed because she was a young bouncy American struggling
against this reserve all the time. Nargess says she tried to fill
the house with fun, and ran into difficulties because Mark
didn't have the same sense of enjoyment.

Then they had a son, Alistair, and for Nargess this changed
things dramatically. 'I now had someone on whom I could
shower my natural ebullience and affection and good nature,
and so Alistair got the full brunt of this and Mark held back
more and more.'

'I felt slightly alienated,' Mark agrees. 'Nargess wasn't
working, and so they were at home all day having fun and I
was out there working in a stressful job.'

Eventually they decided to separate, with Mark moving out.
'I didn't want to leave. What I wanted to do was change

how things had been set up in 1971 and start again. But I didn't know how.'

At this point they divorced and lived apart for three years, seeing each other on the standard fortnightly visit for Mark to see Alistair.

Mark always had a hope that they would get back together. 'For the first time in my life I wanted something but couldn't achieve it,' he admits. Then he was given some ballet tickets, and he called Nargess to ask her to join him.

She was completely surprised: 'It proved to me that Mark had changed. He'd never taken me to the ballet in fifteen years of marriage, so I knew something was up!'

When they decided to marry again, they decided to rewrite the contract between them completely.

'I feel that people set up the rules and the guidelines fairly early on,' Mark says, 'and, whether a husband is looking for a mother figure or a soulmate, you make the guidelines very early, and they are very difficult to change. In fact they are almost impossible to change. I felt that if somehow there was a way to change this radically, breaking it and remoulding it, it could work. And that's what we managed to do.'

'This second marriage has been a huge success,' Nargess adds. 'It's been wonderful to have been able to start again right from day one and go along the path that we wanted to this time. We said that this time we'd talk about everything, nothing would fester, and it's been fantastic and there are no topics we won't talk about.'

Mark and Nargess have now been married for eleven years – second time around.

John Walker's role in his friends' weddings often requires him to take an active role. And no, John's not a vicar. He contacted Home Truths *when he heard a story about being the best woman at a wedding. John's experience is the same, and yet totally different.*

John the Bridesmaid
John Walker, 2003

'Helen and I have been friends since we were about twelve, and when she was choosing her bridesmaids apparently she chose the people who she wanted the most, and she didn't seem to differentiate between boys and girls.'

John, it seems, is cursed – or blessed, depending on your point of view – with the epithet 'honorary girl'. Which basically means he prefers the company of women to the company of men, and always has done. And women feel at ease in his company, neither competing over him nor feeling threatened by his presence.

'They seem to relax in my company and not worry about there being an infiltrator, and I think that's what earned me the title. It was actually a really sweet thing to be asked, I think,' he says of Helen's request. And it didn't even involve him in cross-dressing.

'I got to wear a proper, typical morning suit, but mine matched the bridesmaid's dresses and not the best man's and groom's costumes,' he explains.

The bridesmaids wore red dresses, and, considering the pedigree of these outfits – which are obviously designed to be unspeakably hideous, so the bride looks all the more beautiful – they were for once rather stylish, and the details of John's waistcoat and his handkerchief were all in the same red.

Despite looking dashing in his morning suit, John was still referred to as the John the Bridesmaid. Though he did make a plea for 'bridesmate', it fell on deaf ears and grinning faces – although in retrospect he realizes that that title might have caused even more confusion, particularly with the groom's family.

The wedding itself was of course just the final piece in the marriage jigsaw. Some time before John donned his waistcoat, he had to run the gauntlet of the hen party. Oh yes – he wasn't getting out of that one just because he was a man.

'Early on,' he says, 'there was a terrifying threat when Helen said that I was to organise the hen party. After the blow to the masculinity of being asked to be a bridesmaid, that was the final blow.'

At this point – with the prospect of a night filled with screaming women and the oiled torsos of the obligatory male strippers – John might reasonably have been expected to regret his earlier choices in life and to have developed a hankering for the rugby club. But Helen didn't let him down. Her hen night was a lovely, sensible evening – in a restaurant.

John had seven months to get used to the idea of being Helen's bridesmaid, to understand his duties, to look at the fabric choices . . . Still, it must have been a startling moment when asked to perform a role so resolutely associated with women, or frequently little girls. And, despite John's ease in the company of women, this experience must have taken some getting used to. After all, it's not every day a man is asked to be a bridesmaid.

'I practised by being a maid of honour, at someone else's wedding,' John says, explaining how he got used to the idea.

So John has been a maid of honour *and* a bridesmaid . . .

'This was a good friend of mine, Kim, who lives in Chicago,' he continues. 'We've been friends for about eight years.'

John was a maid of honour with Kim's good friend Amy,

and both of them carried out all the duties associated with that role.

'We stayed over in the hotel room with her the night before the wedding. Which again sounds terrible now I say this . . .'

In case you're wondering, John had the spare bed, and the groom didn't mind. After all, John was the maid of honour. And in the morning Amy and he got Kim up and dressed for her big day, and he even got to make a speech.

'I told the quite embarrassing story of how Kim and I came to know each other. Eight years ago – back when the internet was all fields – we bumped into each other in a chat room. There was a new TV programme on at the time that no one was watching, called *The X Files*, and I chose "Mulder" as my name, and there was someone in the room called "Scully".'

And that was Kim, who paved the way for Helen and the tearing away of those final, flimsy strips of masculinity which led to John achieving the privileged position of being one of the few men – possibly the only man – who can claim to have followed the bride down the aisle. Twice.

An honour indeed. But isn't John a little worried about the classic wedding curse: always a bridesmaid, never a bride?

'Yes, it leads me to those quiet sobbing moments in the evening.'

Well, at least with a morning suit he's got plenty of pockets to stash his tissues – unlike his female colleagues in their more traditional confections.

Marian Rudd has happy memories of her schooldays in Burnley back in the 1920s. They wrote on a slate with chalk, and she remembers learning to plait raffia, which was nailed to the wall.

She and Ron were always top of the form, but they were also the best of pals. They would share what money they had to buy sweets together. Ron remembers Marian as a lovely little girl. She always had a ribbon in her hair and wore a pinny, and she had lovely twinkling eyes.

Smiling Eyes
Marian Rudd, 2002

When they left infant school, Marian and Ron went to different schools, their paths didn't cross, and their lives moved on. More than seventy years later, Ron and his son decided to go to the Lakes for a holiday. They made a stop in Burnley out of sheer nostalgia. Ron remembers they were wandering around a bookshop when his son chanced upon a book, *A Lifetime in Burnley*, and asked his dad if he knew the author: 'Did you ever know Marian Rudd?'

Ron remembered Marian well, but couldn't believe that it was the same one and that she was still alive. However, the shop assistant not only knew Marian but had her phone number.

Marian received a call from Ron that evening. She had no idea who he was, but he sounded genuine and nice, so she agreed to meet him for dinner. Her neighbour couldn't believe she was going. 'I felt a bit of a tart the way she said it!' Marian recalls.

They spent the evening chatting and reminiscing – or trying to: Marian had no memory of Ron, and holding hands. Marian mentioned that she was going on holiday alone to Guernsey in a couple of weeks' time. A few days later Ron rang to ask if she'd object to him meeting her there. They split up from their respective groups and spent their days getting to know each other.

After a holiday in Malta, Ron and Marian decided that they would like to be married. Both now in their eighties, they look forwards to years of happiness, growing into 'funny old sticks' together. It was a good thing Ron and his son took that detour to Burnley.

Some people – naming no names – find remembering to send birthday cards to their dearly beloved ones a hard enough task. So ponder Maggie, who has remembered to send her friend Mike a Valentine's Day card for the last forty years, despite the lack of any romantic link between them.

Funny Valentine
Maggie Chapman, 2003

Maggie Chapman has sent the same man a Valentine's Day card for forty years, although they've never been romantically linked. In her teens, over forty years ago, Maggie liked to send Valentine's Day cards to boys who didn't have girlfriends.

One of the recipients of her cards was Mike, a young bank clerk. Mike managed to work out who sent him the card and, luckily, saw the joke.

The following year, Maggie was surprised to receive a Valentine's Day card from Mike, and they've been exchanging cards ever since.

This has now been going on for forty years, and she's never missed a year – well, almost. One year Maggie did forget. She saw Mike in the street, and he looked quite crestfallen.

And Maggie says one year Mike's card was late and she

thought, 'There was something terribly missing from my life. I thought, "Oh dear, Mike's forgotten me."'

Maggie and Mike very rarely meet. 'We've always had a very easy relationship. When we do see each other, we laugh a lot.'

But there's never been anything more to it than that.

One of the more regular musings on Home Truths *concerned people who miss their offsprings' former boyfriends or girlfriends. Those of you who didn't listen every week, or who regularly wiped the sweat from your brow when the latest inappropriate boyfriend or girlfriend left the house for the last time, might have wondered just what all the fuss was about – good riddance and all that. Perhaps Tamsin and Jo Pierce can illuminate you.*

Tamsin and Jo
Tamsin and Jo Pierce, 2004

Tamsin met her first serious boyfriend at eighteen, but they broke up after a couple of years. Whereas Tamsin got on with things with nary a backward glance, her mother, Jo, grieved over the young man's sudden exit from their lives. Tamsin, giddy with freedom, had no idea that her mother had become so attached to the boyfriend, until she picked up a national newspaper some ten years later. She, Tamsin, sat down to read an article written by a mother about her daughter's ex, and as she read she was overcome by a sense of déjà vu.

'It was about the pain that the mother had felt, and the involvement that the boy had had with the family. It was all very familiar to me, but slightly too much, and as I carried on reading I realized that it wasn't just quite like my life, it actually was my life. It was quite hard to read – it made me cry. And the surname of the writer was my grandmother's maiden name. Now my mother has, over the years, done bits and pieces of journalism. So I got on the phone.'

Tamsin, the newspaper in front of her, challenged her mother over the article, but Jo was somewhat vague in her response, not knowing which week they had planned to run it. When she realized it was published, she was more delighted than remorseful. This only compounded the chagrin Tamsin felt at seeing herself all over a newspaper, and the bewilderment at how involved her mother had felt in the relationship.

'The relationship had been ten years previous to when I was reading it. It was my first big love, and I was eighteen at the time,' Tamsin explains. 'And he became very involved with my family, because he didn't have much involvement in his own.'

Needless to say, the poor chap was totally unsuitable: five years older; jobless; living in a council bedsit in Hackney when Hackney wasn't trendy, just dangerous. And he spent all his time hanging out in a second-hand record shop. Actually, he sounds great – an idler when idling wasn't trendy, just, well, lazy.

Jo first encountered the lad over the breakfast table – a familiar introduction point for parents and the waifs and strays their offspring bring home. She suspects Tamsin was younger than eighteen, because she was still in her school uniform – in fact she'd gone off to school in her uniform, leaving her mother to initiate introductions.

'She'd cleared off to wherever she was going,' Jo tells us. 'There he was in his black outfit with his golden ponytail, and I thought, "Well, I can either say get out or I can say who are you?" And I made myself some toast and tea and sat down and talked to him. He had very courtly manners. He looked quite frightening, but he was a rather gentle person.'

Several months passed, and Tamsin, who was now in her

gap year, wanted to move in with the rockabilly.

'I think Mum and Dad were expecting me to come home, earn a bit of money, and then go on my travels. And in fact I came home, started this relationship, and moved to Hackney with him,' Tamsin explains. 'And that was that, really. And I was there for my whole gap year and then I went to Liverpool University, but our relationship continued for another year.'

With Tamsin in Liverpool, this left Jo free rein to get to know the boyfriend.

'Well, we'd rather taken him to our hearts because he was nice. I remember once we went to a pub and there was some music, and we danced. Her father danced with his daughter, and I danced with the boyfriend.'

But all good things must come to an end, and the dancing down the pub was kiboshed for good one weekend when Tamsin came home from Liverpool and just announced it.

Jo could imagine how painful it would be for the pair of them, and decided to do what she could to soften the blow.

'I thought she was very vulnerable – I thought they both very vulnerable. And I took the decision that that evening I would put the phone outside my bedroom door, because I thought that he would ring. And the phone did go in the middle of the night and I answered it, rather than let her answer it. I think it was one of the saddest phone calls I've ever had. But I said to him, "I think this is the right thing, I don't think you should be talking to her, because I don't want your hopes to be got up, I think she's made the right decision, and I think she knows she has, and I think this is really the end."'

Interfering can be a dangerous strategy, and Jo has always wondered if she did the right thing.

Tamsin's response to her mother's involvement – or meddling, depending on how you view it – is perhaps surprising: 'I don't really feel it's my call. I mean, I was twenty. I didn't expect Mum to field the calls and to be there for him. But then I didn't expect her to because I didn't really pay much attention to the relationship that she had with him.'

Jo decided to write the article because she felt that her mourning of the lost relationship with the rockabilly spoke to a larger issue in the modern world. People have relationships without getting married, and parents become attached to their children's partners but might suddenly lose them.

'And,' she adds, 'he'd become very much a part of us. I don't have sons, and I think we'd rather thought of him as a son.'

Nonetheless, when she wrote the article she didn't think to tell Tamsin, because, although it was very much based in personal experience, it was about something much larger. Not that Tamsin minded too much.

'We just talked about,' Tamsin says. 'And it was nice to see it from somebody else's point of view. And it was quite nice to have been written about, to be honest.'

Looking back on it all, Jo accepts that her relationship with this ex-boyfriend was perhaps a little too intimate, and maybe that was the root of the problem.

'I invested too much in it, and I think he certainly invested too much in our family. When we were talking on the phone that evening, or that night, he said, "Well, I know it was just a silly dream." And I think it was the dream that we all mourned really.'

And, although all their lives have moved on in so many ways since Tamsin dashed out to school that morning ten years ago, there remains a place in Jo's heart for the gentle rockabilly from untrendy Hackney.

'I'm awfully sad about it, yes. Although I know that Tamsin's now living with the right guy and so on and so forth, I will always miss him.'

Monica Grenfell takes a more robust approach to her children's partners than Jo Pierce. Articles in newspapers, musing and mourning, are not for her. She's too busy planning a campaign with military precision to ensure the latest girlfriend doesn't escape, ever. After all, the hapless woman could be mothering Monica's grandchildren.

My Sons' Girlfriends
Monica Grenfell, 2000

Monica gets quite excited when she finds out that a son – Michael, twenty-six, or James, twenty-four – is getting serious about his girlfriend.

'I think I'm going to have this wonderful new person in my life,' Monica admits, adding that her interest is fuelled by her own agenda: 'It's not a suitable wife for my children I'm interested in, but a suitable daughter-in-law for myself!'

James discovered his mother's motives when he introduced his first long-term girlfriend to her, about five years ago.

'Mum rather grilled her, I think,' he remembers.

There's a sharp intake of breath from Monica: 'I didn't do any such thing ... But you have to think, don't you, that a daughter-in-law is for life, not just for Christmas. You want someone who's going to be a really good friend to you – and, of course, on whom you can bestow all your undoubted wisdom!'

The picture is becoming ever clearer.

When Monica's been particularly impressed by a girlfriend, she makes sure on the second visit that she pulls out all the stops. 'It's a bit like having a home visit from the RSPCA. You want to make sure they're going to like you and that you're a family they'll be happy to come and visit for years.'

Overprotective? Interfering?

'Yes,' affirms Monica. 'Absolutely. And I'm very happy to be so.'

Monica herself has remarried, and her main concern was that the man she chose would be a good stepfather to her two sons: 'Anything we do has a ripple effect on everyone else's life. I think it's important, if someone's coming into the family as a daughter-in-law, to have good relations with everyone.'

It's not too difficult to imagine Monica having a ripple effect.

James has learned – he didn't say if it was the hard way or not – that when his mum is keen on a particular girlfriend 'She makes that bit extra effort.'

Perhaps too much?

'Well – yes. Mum sets the agenda for it all. She takes it quite seriously.'

Whereas the boys behave with all the laidback casualness one expects of young men – the RSPCA inspector being a long way from their minds.

Monica is, according to her son James, a bit of a looker, very glamorous and very fit, and that can be a bit of a threat to new girls coming into the house. That and the barrage of questions . . .

The brothers can tell when Monica approves of a particular girlfriend, because the endless probing questions dry up.

'I'm just dying for a lovely daughter-in-law,' Monica admits. 'I want that relationship in my life. The first time round, having your own children, it was all such a rush. I want a daughter-in-law who'll be a good friend, someone I can get to like. Someone who won't just see me as the older figure.'

'And I always thought you were thinking of us, Mum!' James adds wryly.

Now, James has been seeing Chloe for about nine months.

'She's older than James,' Monica says, 'and has a child – which threw me completely.'

Monica admits she had this picture of herself – which doesn't perturb her at all – as the mother-in-law from hell, with a daughter she could boss around, giving her all the advice she doesn't want when she has Monica's first grandchild.

Still, Chloe has her plus points, and Monica has clearly zeroed in on her.

'She's also about six foot tall. But she's fabulous, fabulous. I'll kill him if he get's rid of her – she just can't go!'

James, you've been warned.

Suzanne Cohen's story is one of how love found a way through the uncertain hand of coincidence, twenty years after she and her eventual husband first met...

Marriage Coincidence
Suzanne and David Cohen, 2004

When Suzanne was fourteen she was dating an older boy, Mike, who was seventeen. Occasionally his friend Dave would tag along. The three of them were part of the Jewish community, and had plenty of opportunity to socialize at youth clubs and dances. And while the three of them were at one of these functions, Suzanne was stealing glimpses at Dave.

'I've got one picture in my mind that's very clear,' Suzanne says. 'We were sat round a table – I think it was in my parent's house – and I just looked at him and I can still remember his face and his smile, thinking he was gorgeous.'

Which was a problem, because the plan was for Suzanne to become engaged to Mike on her sixteenth birthday. But things didn't work out.

'I thought no, that was just too much for me.'

So, now Suzanne was a free agent and Dave could move in.

185

But was it appropriate to do so with Mike being his mate? And how would he go about it?

'I think we were at a dance and she wasn't with Mike any more, so I asked her out. I thought that was the right time to do it,' Dave remembers.

Anyway, Suzanne and Dave had a couple of dates, but the spark they'd both imagined wasn't there, and they went their separate ways until they met again at Salford Tech in 1977, and again they went on some dates – 'On and off dates,' Suzanne explains.

Dave started working in 1979, so they'd meet up around the university precinct. And again they went on the odd date here and the odd date there, but again it never developed into a relationship – which seems extraordinary, given where they are now.

'Well, the thing I remember', Suzanne says, 'was the first time he finished with me because he didn't have enough money to take me out. And I was so upset, saying, "I'll pay, I'll pay." But that didn't work out. And then the second time I was wanting to go to university, I was wanting to get out of Manchester.'

Suzanne first went to Bradford University and then York, and then moved down to London to get a job. Dave, meanwhile, was working in Reading – no doubt pining for Suzanne, you're thinking.

'I have to admit,' Dave says sheepishly – 'this isn't going to sound very good – I don't think I did actually think about her.'

Oh. But maybe Suzanne was thinking about Dave.

'Well, I used to think about David from time to time. And when I moved down to London I had to clear out my rooms at home and I was looking for David's phone number, because I just had this urge or desire to contact him. But it wasn't there, sadly. And then I thought, "Well, I'll try and find him," and I got all the telephone books for Manchester and I found a few

David Cohens, but I just stopped from phoning the numbers.'

Well, she couldn't phone all of them, could she? So Suzanne kept working, waiting for Mr Right to turn up so they could buy a flat and start a life. Then, at thirty-two, she realized that it wasn't going to happen. She'd answered some ads in the personal columns, but mostly she had been single. As had Dave. So then she decided to take positive action and put an ad in *Time Out*.

'I went to bed one night, and this perfect ad – it felt as though it was dictated to me – came into my mind, and I had to get up and write it down.'

> Jewish woman 32, spiritual, passionate, intelligent, imaginative seeks male soulmate, 28–38, to share the highs and lows of life's lessons.

Suzanne got around thirty replies, weeded out the loonies, and went on some dates. Meanwhile, David was replying to ads – although he was getting a bit worn down by it all.

'Then I decided to concentrate only on Jewish people,' David takes up the story, 'and this one appealed to me. The highs and lows – there's certainly been a few of those. And "soulmate" appealed to me. And I wrote a letter.'

Their first conversation must have been bizarre, after all that time – assuming, of course, that they recognized each other.

'Well, it went very well,' Suzanne recalls. 'And we chatted and everything, and then we had Manchester in common and things like that. But I didn't recognize David's voice at all. And then, after we'd agreed to meet, he said, "What's your surname?" So I gave him my surname. And then I asked Dave for his, and it was Cohen, and I thought, "What – Dave Cohen?" And my whole body just shook and trembled. I thought, "It can't be. It can't be."'

'Also, you mentioned . . . you asked me who I knew in Manchester,' Dave adds.

'That's it. So I waited to see if he mentioned Mike, then obviously you were the Dave Cohen that I knew.'

And then Suzanne told him they'd been out before.

On their first date, Dave arranged it so he would just appear – a rather cinematic, Harry Lime sort of entrance – instead of emerging slowly through the crowds.

'Yes, it was something like out of a film. And Suzanne had a black top on. I can't remember what I was wearing, but I certainly remember what Suzanne had on.'

That first date lasted twelve hours, and made the pair of them wonder why they'd broken up previously.

'I was just so happy that we'd met,' Suzanne says. 'I mean, it was like a dream come true to have remembered David and to have always thought about him and thought "Oh, if only we could . . . what would have happened." And then to have met him again was just incredible.'

Was this sense of ecstasy mutual?

'I don't know if I felt exactly the same,' David bravely admits.

Clearly not one given to flights of fancy or a colourful turn of phrase our David. Still, he knew he'd met – or should that be remet? – someone special, and after the second date, as he so poetically puts it, 'That was it.'

When Harold met Jackie he was sixty-one and she was fourteen. He's now ninety-nine, she's fifty-three, and their next wedding anniversary will be their thirty-first.

When Harold Met Jackie . . .
Harold and Jackie, 1998

'We met in church,' says Harold. 'I got to know her very well while my first wife was alive. Being the vicar, I was in touch with most people, and Jackie was the organist so she came into the vestry every week. After my first wife died, in 1965, I continued to depend upon Jackie for many parish things. Then, later on, I realized she meant more to me. We married two years later.'

Despite her feelings for Harold, it wasn't an easy decision for Jackie to make.

'I thought, "I must be mad marrying somebody that much older than me." So I applied to do Voluntary Services Overseas. Then, when I was accepted, I took fright and thought, "Oh no, I can't go away and leave him for a year."'

The couple married in 1968, when Harold was sixty-eight and Jackie was twenty-two. Their marriage caused a sensation in the tabloid press, but Jackie enjoyed the support of her friends, who all approved of Harold and saw how well the couple got on together.

'It was a bit different in the parish,' Jackie remembers, with some understatement. 'Nobody actually said anything to our faces, but three people left the church, never to come again.'

Once Harold's daughters from his first marriage, all of whom were quite a bit older than Jackie, had recovered from the initial shock, they reacted well to their father's remarriage. Two years later, Harold and Jackie had a son, who's due to become a father himself soon.

'There's only two things we fight over,' says Jackie. 'One is planning routes to go anywhere, because he's been driving since Noah left the ark and thinks he knows every road. The other is gardening, because Harold knows absolutely nothing about gardening and a couple of times he's been out and pruned things in my absence and got shouted at!'

That sounds much like any other couple, regardless of age. However, the difference in Jackie and Harold's ages has had consequences which have become more marked with age. Jackie describes their marriage as a 'seesaw'. In the early days, when she was just twenty-two, she used to depend on him for a lot. Now the roles have completely reversed as Harold approaches his hundredth year, with him becoming completely dependent on her.

To a lot of people their age difference might seem an impossible burden, particularly in these later years, but, as Jackie and Harold have ably illustrated, love doesn't discriminate and can overcome whatever challenges are put in its path.

8

A Four-Legged Friend, or Sometimes Two

Home Truths listeners with long memories might still be wondering who, why, when and where the cats were wearing lifejackets, following an offhand remark by a contributor that tantalizingly was left hanging and remains suffused in an air of mystery to this day.

There is little mystery, on the other hand, about the matter of tree frogs driving traction engines – an image conjured up in a moment of whimsy, with absolutely no basis in reality other than a one-time mayor of Valparaiso, one Hector Pinto, who enjoyed, or endured, the nickname Tree Frog. And, apparently the nickname was entirely appropriate. Did Hector have a vivid green complexion? The answer is out there somewhere – along with the story of a stuffed dog, thoughts about cat sniffing, and sundry tales about rabbits which have obsessed listeners over the years. But we're going to start our selection with birds of a different feather.

Andy Barber is a magician, cartoonist and keen local historian in his native Bungay, Suffolk, and is unsurprisingly enthusiastic to maintain local traditions. You might imagine that these include brewing, observing festivals associated with the new moon, and samphire picking. But you'd be wrong, because Andy's principal passion is for chickens – and not just any old chickens either.

Chicken Roundabout

Andy Barber, 2005

'It's probably the only thing that makes Bungay particularly interesting really,' Andy candidly admits. And that thing is a traffic island populated by about forty cockerels and one hen. If life isn't precarious enough for the lone hen, given such a disparity in numbers, she adds to life's dangers by perching somewhat precariously right in the top boughs of one of the trees.

The chickens have been in their current, unusual, home for nearly fifty years, having spread from a smallholding nearby in the days before the roundabout. Recently the council tried to eradicate them – like feathered Chagos Islanders – but, as Andy pointed out, there was a bit of an outcry.

'A bunch of locals who love the chickens got together and said, "We've got to try and make some sort of statement here." The protest gig, on the roundabout, actually helped prevent that eradication.'

Mysteriously, however, some of the chickens had disappeared in the fracas. 'It was all rather strange,' Andy continued, as if nothing else about this story was, 'because there were a lot of chickens, and then suddenly the council turned up and the roundabout – which had been covered in gorse, hedges and loads of brush – was cleared. And the chickens just disappeared. So perhaps they've been hen-napped, which I think is a possibility, to keep the population down.

'There are all sorts of stories,' Andy adds mysteriously. 'Some people think they were liberated because they're a special breed of chicken on Chicken Roundabout.'

A bit – you might say – like the creatures on the Galapagos Islands which, separated from all other breeds, develop their own strain. Which makes you wonder if other animals inhabit the roundabout, and, if not, why not?

'Well, there's the mysterious black rabbit, which has appeared again. He disappeared for a while, and then he came back,' Andy adds, creating an air of mystery. 'I think he's a sort of James Bond Blofeld character at Chicken Roundabout. He seems to be in control of the chickens. He's kind of separate,' Andy continues, warming to his theme. 'He keeps away from the chickens, but you can tell that he's kind of in control in a strange sort of way. It's quite possible that underneath Chicken Roundabout he's built a sort of missile-base-cavern-type affair, from where he's running the roundabout – or even the whole of Bungay.'

The mind boggles at the possibilities. Perhaps he's put implants into the chickens' brains. Extraordinary to think of in itself, but, given the rabbit's lack of opposable thumbs, quite a feat of dexterity, let alone ingenuity. Maybe he's trained the chickens to go into space and release chicken droppings all over the world unless he's given £10,000 million tomorrow?

On balance, Andy's not so sure: 'Well, I think you're being silly now.'

So, if you're heading down the A143 towards Great Yarmouth, for instance, take a look out for the chickens. If you're there at dawn you'll hear a fearful chorus of cock-a-doodle-dooing. Power to the poultry indeed, for the beaks shall inherit the earth.

We've all had a frog in our throats, but how many of us can say we've had a toad in our trainer? John Ward can. And before any of you start thinking, 'Oh yes, I've found a toad in my shoe – the shoe I left out in the garden, overnight, when it rained,' bear this in mind: John's toad may have hopped into his shoe at home, but he didn't hop out for another nine thousand miles.

A Toad in My Trainer

John Ward, 1998

John has the kind of job where he has to be ready to travel at short notice. And the call duly came to leap on a plane to China. So out came the suitcase.

'The last thing I packed were my trainers, which I normally keep in the garage. I kick them off there, and leave them to fester. I snatched them up and threw them in the top of the suitcase,' John remembers. 'When I got to Beijing, I opened my suitcase and a toad popped out of my trainer – a live toad! I suppose it had crawled into my trainer in the garage. It had survived a nine-hour flight in who knows what sort of temperatures, and there it was – a big smile on its face.'

Not to put too fine a point on it, the discovery made John jump a mile.

'I sort of parked the toad in the corner of the room and trapped it in the trainer, using the other shoe.'

However, when John returned from work the trainers had been put in the wardrobe by the maid, and, despite a thorough search of the room, the web-toed stowaway had vanished.

Concerned for the toad's well-being, and reinstatement of his only link with home, John called the floor manager of the hotel. Explaining the problem wasn't easy. The floor manager's English was as spasmodic as John's Mandarin. And an attempt to draw the toad sent the man backing out of the room.

However, the next day John found the toad crawling around the skirting boards of his bedroom. He might have eluded the attention of the maid, but now the toad faced another problem: sustenance.

'I wasn't really sure what toads ate,' John explained, 'so I got a salami and salad sandwich from the restaurant.' What made John think salami was a natural food for toads isn't clear. Still, it was probably a better choice than a plate of crispy aromatic duck.

John stuffed the sandwich into the airline overnight bag in which the toad had set up camp, thoughtfully adding some moist cotton wool to keep him comfortable.

On the afternoon of the third day the toad ceased to move. So maybe John's culinary choices weren't so on the mark after all. He was worried. But after a few fretful hours the toad revived. He was probably still jet-lagged. And John took him on one final journey – not in the trainer – to a new home.

'I set it free in this exclusive villa compound in northern Beijing, with an ornamental lake and rocks. He seemed quite happy – he still had that smile that toads have.'

The toad to Beijing . . .

People do dote on their animals, but perhaps a bridge too far had been crossed when a certain Beryl Fahey came on to the programme to talk about her lack of a sense of smell. The interview went off piste, and the nation was introduced to a hitherto rather furtive pastime.

Pet Sniffing
Beryl Fahey, 2004

'I always enjoyed smells, and when I was a kid one of the first things I discovered was that other people's houses smelled different and other people's bread and butter tasted different,' Beryl said, explaining her acute sense of regret at the loss of her sense of smell – a sense that in Beryl seems to have been remarkably well calibrated.

Everyone who can smell, of course, has a favourite smell,

and smells can conjure up a variety of delightful memories and sensations. Beryl had a handful of wistfully remembered scent experiences.

'Well, things like smelling wood smoke . . .'

You can almost smell it now, can't you? A crackling fire – warm and inviting.

'Or when you go out on a nice frosty morning . . .'

Ah yes, the crisp air – as if you're the first person in the world to breathe it in.

'Or the smell of the cat when it's been lying in the sun . . .'

What? Hold on!

'I don't know, perhaps I'm a bit weird smelling my cat,' Beryl added, some might say redundantly.

Still . . . Perhaps if you rub your face in their face, that might be quite nice.

'Yeah, that's right – it's nice,' Beryl quickly agreed. 'It's a nice smell, and things like that have all gone now.'

Mind you, you'd have to pick the right cat to do it. Some would not stand for that sort of behaviour.

'Well, ours are rather lazy and passive,' Beryl countered.

Cats – even if they are lazy and passive – you never really own them, do you? Let alone when you've got a bunch of stroppy, country cats.

'No,' Beryl agreed, adding, 'They'd consider it a liberty wouldn't they?'

Which is absolutely true. Because, just as you don't feel you own them, they absolutely feel they own you.

Well, this was the tip of the iceberg, and before Home Truths *had the chance to sniff out the difference between the coat of a greyhound and the feathers of a cockatoo we were inundated with listeners' accounts of their own pet sniffing, or pet owner's therapy . . .*

Sheila Mortlock phoned in this contribution: 'From childhood I'd loved sniffing our dogs' coats, especially when they were wet, which is a reversal of the usual dogs' habit. Now that I'm dogless and we've become a cat family I now sniff our cat.'

Isn't that some sort of pet apostasy? From dog to cat? The kind of behaviour that in the Reformation might have seen the sniffer hanged, drawn and quartered?

'Oh,' Sheila continued, 'and I also love sniffing wool jumpers. Does that make me odd? I thought everyone had something they liked to sniff. I'm sure that this could be a rich source of psychological research.'

A rich source of something . . . In fact we've already carried out that psychological research, but before we reveal the explosive results that will set the nation talking it might be advisable to solicit an ally, so here's Bev Thomas, who'd rung up in disgust at the mention of cat sniffing.

'The warmed cat that you have to sniff, I mean that was just too much. You know, my husband and I were washing up the breakfast things, enjoying our morning, and we just went to pieces really – sort of "Urghh, how could they?"'

Bev's repugnance, both rational and rather heartfelt set us wondering if she'd had unpleasant experiences with cats in the past?

'Yes I have, yes – which I'd like to draw a veil over really, because they were so bad.'

Well, that was just too tempting. Perhaps Bev would spell it out . . .

'A certain cat got stuck in our house overnight, and did certain things on my son's duvet.'

Which, on balance, was probably spelt out enough, particularly when you consider the time *Home Truths* was broadcast in the morning. Still, that was just one cat. No need to tar them all with the same brush, is there? We wondered if Bev ever took a shine to other cats?

'No, not at all.'

Oh.

'They're completely disdainful of human beings,' Bev added brusquely.

However, other listeners didn't agree. The switchboard was ablaze with calls from passionate pet sniffers with useful tips and lovingly told anecdotes. One fan of this pastime, Kate Kellan, suggested smelling your cat when it's been in the garden. That way you get a heady mixture (her words, not ours, by the way) of fresh grass and fresh cat – absolutely gorgeous.

Erica, from Twickenham, was hugely relieved to discover she wasn't alone in her cat-sniffing habit.

Yes, Erica, there are others out there in the great, wide galaxy. It's not just you . . . Her cat, Scampy, is rather old and decrepit, and getting very stinky in between sponge baths . . .

Sponge baths? Does she – I hear you ask – take Scampy's temperature on a regular basis and stand around its basket looking at its charts?

Anyway, back to the sponge baths – because at her advanced age Scampy needs help with her ablutions. During the day the cat sleeps under the duvet, and when Erica comes home she often sticks her head under it and inhales.

Only if she's stressed though.

I wonder what Bev would make of that?

'Well, I'm horrified by the duvet one. I knew there would be a duvet one. I was trying to prepare myself for that one, and that to me is just sacrilege, because to me the bed is the sacred place, you know – I don't want anything in it catty. The idea of having a cat . . . Oh no, no.'

*

The madness doesn't stop at cats, apparently. Here's what Fiona Firth in Leicestershire enjoys imbibing.

'If you think cat smelling is wonderful,' Fiona gushes, 'I tell you there is nothing quite as wonderful as sniffing a warm Dalmatian. They do smell wonderfully biscuity, and quite unlike any other dogs.'

Mmmm, biscuity ... Like a fine wine – biscuity, with a hint of blackberry and a strong finish. Dalmatians grown on the southern slopes, bathed by the sun ... I wonder what Bev thinks?

'I'm sorry, you're taking me to places I don't want to go.'

It's extraordinary stuff, so passionately told.

'It is, yes, and they're so emphatic.'

And there are so many of them.

Our next encounter with wildlife involves travel – though nothing as exotic as a toad's trip to Beijing. It begins on one of those irritating and confusing three-lane roads, where the middle lane is meant for overtaking.

Ray Lyon, with no members of the constabulary in sight, was travelling down his own three-lane road, on his way to work, when something strange happened. And, in case you were wondering, no animals were sniffed in the events described below.

Rodent Rage
Ray Lyon, 1998

'I had this feeling that a dog was trying to overtake me,' Ray explains. 'Instead of looking round, my first instinct was to look down at the speedometer. I was doing at least 50 m.p.h. I thought, "It must be a greyhound!"'

What was happening did involve an animal, but not a dog.

Not even a greyhound – which, although swift, isn't really built for middle- or long-distance running.

'Instead of a dog overtaking me on the outside of the car, it was a mouse sat on the windowsill on the inside of the car.'

As Ray turned, the mouse leaped from the window on to his right shoulder and scuttled across his chest, down to his thigh, and along his thigh, before diving into the well of his car. As quickly as he could, Ray pulled over and crawled around trying to find it. Cue plenty of jokes about taking the rat run to work and back, although for Ray it was no laughing matter.

'The mouse could be anywhere,' Ray realized – 'inside the seats, or back in the engine compartment. So I thought the only solution was to tuck my trousers into my socks and continue my journey.'

After all, there wasn't a stool for him to stand on.

Later that day Ray returned home, with his trousers still well tucked in against the errant mouse. In the hope of dealing humanely with the situation, he left his car in his garage with the door open and a plank leading to the ground as a hint that the mouse should leave.

After a few days without any rodent interference, Ray, thinking the mouse had gone, untucked his trousers from his socks – like Icarus flying so close to the sun – and started on his journey.

'The mouse leaped out and hit me on the shin, and I realized it was still around.'

The mouse attack was decisive for Ray. His car wasn't big enough for the both of them. One of them had to go – and it wasn't going to be the man with his trousers tucked into his socks.

'I bought a trap. The next morning I went to the car, and there it was – dead. And that is the end of the mouse story.'

Jeff Berens risked ridicule and mocking laughter to reveal his terrifying ordeal at the hoofs of a flock of hooligan sheep . . .

Nasty Sheep
Jeff Berens, 2001

'I used to walk my dog Tryffan a couple of times a day,' Jeff explains.

By way of background detail, it's worth mentioning that Tryffan is a cross between a black Labrador and a corgi. Not, on balance, an obvious crossbreed – the practicalities of how it might even have come about make the mind boggle. Still, the outcome is a very, very large and very, very temperamental dog.

'I lived in the Pennines above Burnley,' Jeff continues. 'Across a field from my house was the countryside. One wet and windy day, Tryffan and I were maybe half a mile from home coming down a long, hilly field. Not much goes on there other than sheep farming – there's hundreds and hundreds of sheep everywhere you look.'

Nothing unusual there.

'I suddenly noticed the sheep seemed to be moving generally towards me,' Jeff continues. 'They were still quite a way off – a few hundred yards. But then I noticed more and more heading down. And then I noticed sheep in the lower part of the field were heading up towards me. The ones I'd walked past, just behind me, they were starting to head towards me as well. All of a sudden I was surrounded by a lot of sheep.'

At this point it seems pertinent to mention that Jeff swears that he wasn't wearing anything unusual or especially provocative to sheep.

'They could have thought it was the farmer bringing them

food. Anyway, I got worried,' he confesses, undeterred. 'The dog was very hard to hold on to. I was worried he'd start running at the sheep – but the sheep didn't seem to be worried by the dog, which isn't normal behaviour for sheep!'

Unless, of course, they knew he was a corgi in Labrador's clothing.

'It was almost like a scene from the film *Zulu*,' Jeff says drily – 'with all the warriors surrounding me. I thought, "I've got to get out of this!" Anyone watching from a distance, at that point, would have seen a chap with a dog running hell for leather being pursued by a lot of sheep.'

And you might think they'd start laughing at the sight. But these weren't namby-pamby, southern-softie, metrosexual sheep.

'They're quite big actually. These aren't softie sheep. They're tough Pennine sheep.'

Hmm.

'As I ran towards the wall at the end of the field, they gave way a little bit. They never quite surrounded me – I didn't let that happen. I might not be here if I had.' Sounding a just a tad defensive, Jeff goes on, 'This is a ridiculous thought. I know sheep don't eat people. I know they don't trample people. But, you know . . .'

Friends, it turns out, weren't especially sympathetic when Jeff let them in on his dark secret. He freely admits it's not something he talks about much at job interviews, and he believes his ex-partner may have lost some respect for him when he unburdened his soul.

Manfully denying any overreaction on his part, Jeff concludes firmly, 'I still think being surrounded by hundreds of sheep is quite intimidating. I've not been walking in that part of the world for a long time. Maybe at the back of my mind I'm thinking they'll get me next time.'

The sheep horror deepens . . .

No one would blame you for thinking that Jeff Berens's story owed something to an overactive imagination. But, like so many other stories on Home Truths, *it spawned more accounts along the same lines.*

So, pass the mint sauce – the sheep are gathering on the horizon in preparation for another attack of fluffily brutal proportions . . .

'My husband and I were out walking with a Labrador,' says Angela Weaver. 'We went into a field containing sheep. My husband was quite some way ahead, because I always stop to look at wildflowers and things, and I saw the sheep start to look really interested. And then gradually they got into a big group, and in the end the whole field of sheep were following along behind my husband, getting closer and closer. The dog got really anxious.'

And, before you ask, it wasn't a crossbreed with a corgi.

'I rather think it might be the dog that's interesting to the sheep. Maybe they're used to having dogs running around behind them, driving them, and they can't understand it walking ahead of them . . .'

Well, it's a theory, Angela.

Mrs Handy contacted *Home Truths* to join the ranks of sheepophobes with this encounter of what can only be described as mutant mutton:

'Donkey's years ago, my daughter and I were faced by what looked like threatening sheep. They were very tall – as tall as we were (I'm five foot). They had thin black legs, long black necks, and black faces, and they were all facing us in a corner of a field where there's a public footpath where we were walking a chihuahua at the time. And we just dared not go through

them – they looked so fierce. Maybe they were just question-
ing . . .'

Maybe, maybe . . .

*Breaking the ice with strangers can be difficult, but
according to the dog owners and walkers in one of London's
parks, who chatted to Frank Wilson, a dog can help you to
make new friends.*

Doggy Friends
Frank Wilson, 1998

For the last twenty-two years 'The Major' has been walking in
a London park with his three Labrador dogs, and, thanks to
the influence of his four-legged companions, in that time he
and they have made many friends.

'In a walk around the park I speak to at least twenty-five
people,' he says. 'Mind you, when you've got three Labradors
it's rather ostentatious publicity.'

Enid agrees that she too has made friends because of her
dog. 'I got him when he was nine months old. I brought him to
the park, and within a week I knew hundreds of people, literally. Dogs are much more sociable, less class-inclined.
Pedigrees don't just walk with pedigrees – they all muck in
together.'

Another dog walker, Steve, has three dogs of his own, and
says they have broken the ice for him many times since his
move to London eighteen months ago. 'It's got a lot to do with
the social behaviour of your dog and the other person's dog. If
the dogs gel, you'll find every time you come to the park the
two dogs will run up to each other like lost friends, and
humans don't have any other choice but to start talking to
each other if their dogs are haring around together.'

Beverley Cuddy of *Dogs Today* magazine agrees with Steve: 'Dogs don't know social etiquette at all, and they do the sort of things that people want to do but haven't got the guts to. Dogs are straight in there – and they are not like that just with other dogs; they're like that with people. Somebody once said dogs allow us to be children again, allow us to play. You can't act the way you do with your dog without the dog, or you'd get locked up.'

But Beverley did point out that, although dogs often bring people together, they can also drive them apart: 'People often split up because of their dogs. Often dog lovers have a dog and the person they meet has a dog, and, while they love each other, the dogs hate each other, and neither will give up their dogs.'

Man's best friend or the named other party in divorce proceedings. It's not always easy being a dog.

One dog that definitely fits into the category of best friend is Bandit. Stephen Markham was born with a heart defect. By the time he was twelve he was spending more and more time in hospital. Regular visits from a special dog who called in to see patients in hospital cheered Stephen immensely. As a result, when he left hospital his mum, Sue, bought him a Lhasa apso. She was called Bandit, and played a very important part in what was to be the last year of Stephen's life.

Stephen's Remarkable Dog
Jessica Markham, 2000

'Bandit used to lie there all day and all night if she had to,' Jessica, Stephen's seventeen-year-old sister, recalls. 'She'd be there for him to stroke, but she'd never put herself in his face, like she would with others – she was very sensitive to his situation.'

Bandit helped Stephen in ways the family could not.

'Stephen thought the family was always judging him and wondering why he didn't do things to help himself,' Sue says, 'but the dog never asked questions. The dog was there for Stephen and for no other reason.'

'Stephen would be very, very ill,' Jessica adds. 'No one quite understood what was wrong – and he didn't know. He'd get very agitated, not talk to us about it at all – but it was a real comfort to know that the dog was with him. She was there for him when he wouldn't let us be.'

Inevitably, Stephen's parents spent a lot of time with their son in hospital, which was very difficult for Jessica and her other brother, because Stephen was ill and they were denied their parents' attention.

'Bandit was helpful – it sounds really sad – as someone there to talk to! When you've got someone really ill in your family, you feel you can't unburden yourself on your parents, because they've got so many other things to worry about. If you're really upset, the dog is always there for you.'

Jessica is preparing herself for the inevitability of Bandit's death – something she dreads, in part because of the role the dog has played in her life, but mostly because the dog became so strongly associated with Stephen.

'It will be another part of losing Stephen – something that meant a lot to him. At the time he died, she lay by his bed for two weeks, howling and crying, waiting for him to come back.'

Sue feels that the whole family benefited from Bandit's presence. Aside from being gravely ill, Stephen was also very non-communicative – a typical teenager really. Still, it was a combination that constantly worried and frustrated his mother.

'He wasn't telling me, and therefore I couldn't help him.

Somehow, the dog was always there and would put a smile on my face when I saw no reason to smile!'

Moreover, Bandit could do for Stephen what others found difficult.

'He forgot for a while that he was ill with the dog,' Jessica remembers. 'The dog treated him as she did everyone else. Stephen wanted to be treated as a normal teenager, and Bandit understood that.'

Sometime after Stephen had died, Sue decided to take Bandit to visit hospitals, thinking perhaps she could do for other children what she'd done for Stephen. Zoe, who is paralysed from the neck down and only has feeling in her face, sees Bandit regularly.

'I put Bandit next to her face, so she can feel her,' Sue explains.

'When she comes in she brightens my day up,' says Zoe.

And her mum, Pearl, says, 'She brightens her up – you can see it in her eyes. She becomes the Zoe prior to the injury. It puts a bit of Zoe back into Zoe.'

And, to end this chapter, here's a piece of advice should you ever find yourself in a zoo, or indeed the desert, confronted with a dromedary.

Giving a Camel the Hump
Jenny Leonard, 2005

Jenny Leonard called to say that one day she had had the *Concise Oxford Turkish Dictionary* in front of her. Browsing through it, she had found the word 'uhklamuk', for which the meaning is 'cry used to make a camel kneel'. She was rather taken by the word, and a couple of months later was in London Zoo and found herself by the camels' enclosure and thought she'd try it out. So she stood by the bars and exclaimed 'Uhk' to the camel nearest her. To her astonishment, the camel – with an air of weariness and irritation – very slowly knelt down. And stayed there. And very slowly Jenny slunk away, and for all she knows the camel's kneeling still.

9

You Need Friends

Unlikely, lifelong, loyal, treacherous, royal – friends of all hues populated Home Truths *stories over the years. And, if you were wondering who the monarchical mate was, well, according to several contributors over the years it was Haile Selassie.*

Kim and Selena were both victims of childhood sexual abuse. Both were successful career women; both had happy second marriages, and children. In spite of this, they continued to experience problems related to what happened to them as children. Eventually Kim founded a small self-help group called Survivors, which is where she and Selina finally met. Their friendship transformed their lives.

A Celebration of Friendship
Kim and Selina, 2001

'Kim stood out. It was an aura she had. She was special, and we just connected because we understand each other,' begins Selina.

Kim says of Selina, 'It was love at first sight. I love her like a sister. Ours is a friendship – but it was love at first sight, in a non-sexual way.'

Kim was first abused, by her grandfather, when she was six years old. The abuse continued until she was eleven.

'Things were dealt with very differently then. Keeping quiet was the better option. It was a family decision, rather than mine,' she recalls.

Kim wasn't allowed to visit her grandfather on her own, but as a family there were still the weekend visits to go through, and family celebrations. Kim felt very alone: 'I thought there was something wrong with me because such a horrible thing had happened.' After the death of her grandfather, Kim thought she would be released from her feelings, but they persisted.

Selina began to be sexually abused by her father when she was eleven. It continued until she was seventeen.

'I never told anyone about the abuse when it was happening. I just knew that I wasn't to say anything. I kept it inside me. I didn't want to upset anybody.'

Kim met and married Mick, and they still have a strong and happy marriage. When her first child was born, she began to feel almost paranoid with the concern that something was going to happen to him. Eventually she went to her doctor and explained that she thought her feelings were connected with her childhood.

Selina, too, found herself struggling with her feelings when her two daughters were children. 'I found it very difficult to hug them. It was as if there was a brick wall between us. I knew it shouldn't be like that.'

Both Selina and Kim received counselling. It was of enormous help, providing Selina with the strength to take her father to court.

'I needed to be believed that it was his fault, not mine. I still felt I was missing out on my life,' she explains.

He was found guilty. But there was still a void.

Kim, too, felt that, after her counselling was complete, she still needed something more. And, fortuitously, it was about this time that the two women met.

'I can remember the first time I saw Selina at the Survivors organization,' says Kim, 'There's always a part of me that feels separate, apart from other people. That's why it was such a wonderful experience meeting Selina – I found a soulmate.'

For Selina, too, it was a meeting which changed her life.

'Kim's so strong. She listens, and makes me laugh – which helps. I began to say things I wanted to say, rather than not say them. I'm me now. Before, I was another person.'

In fact Selina's influence helped Kim regain the childhood she felt she'd never had. 'It's silly to most people,' Kim says, 'but we play on the swings, go to the funfair – I missed out so much. It's like a second childhood. I wouldn't have been able to do it by myself, but I can do it with Selina.'

Selina and Kim's friendship had an impact on their marriages. Both husbands were understandably cautious and curious about this powerful new relationship in their wives' lives, but both have come to see the incredibly positive impact the friendship has had on all of them.

'It's taken time for my husband to understand the relationship Selina and I have,' says Kim. 'We love each other dearly, but Selina and I also have a special relationship. He acknowledges that Selina has been a big help to me, and says I'm a more interesting person because of that!'

Selina's husband and family also noticed a difference in her behaviour. 'My husband once said, "Who is the real you?" I think now he sees the real me. I'm more confident, and tend to stand my ground more.'

The memories are still exactly that – receding, but ever present – and there are times when both women feel dragged down by them. But, whereas in the past neither felt she had someone to turn to or could express how she felt, now Kim knows she will always have Selina, and Selina knows she will always have Kim.

Caught in the Soho pub bombing in London in April 1999,
Gary Reid sustained serious injuries. Gary, who is gay, is
still in a wheelchair, and unable to return to work as a
psychiatric nurse. Instead, he has had to rely heavily on the
support of friends and family, as well as the help of
professionals. One such professional is Rosemary Drewery,
a Metropolitan Police family liaison officer. Her police role
is officially at an end now, but the two have remained close
friends.

An Unofficial Friendship
Gary Reid, 2001

'My injuries made it hard for people to recognize me,' Gary
says, remembering the immediate aftermath of the bombing.
'The only way they could identify me was by my tattoo. My
dad described me as looking like something out of a monster
movie.'

Gary was in intensive care in a coma for several weeks. He
had to have one leg amputated below the knee, his arm was
shattered, and his eardrum was perforated.

Rosemary had seen Gary many times before he saw her.
'He seemed to lie there for ever,' she says. 'At times we didn't
think we'd see him on the next visit. He was covered in ban-
dages. My first impression was that he was a middle-aged man
with a big round face.'

Gary first saw Rosemary as she sat talking with another
patient. 'I remember thinking, "What an attractive-looking
woman!" – not at all my idea then of the police. One day she
visited in her uniform. It didn't look like her at all. She was
wearing men's shoes. "For God's sake!" I said. "What are
they?"'

Gary and Rosemary got on from the start. Their relationship was based then on Rosemary's work as a family liaison

officer. An important part of this was to prepare Gary for his time in court.

'Things would come out at the trial which might have upset him,' says Rosemary. 'I wanted to be there to support him.'

'Being in court was part of the process of taking away the feeling of "Why me?"' Gary says, explaining why going to the trial of the bomber was so important to him. 'And I wanted to see what type of a guy he was. Rosemary was like my big sister guiding me through the reporters literally chasing us down the street. I felt protected by her.'

Normally a police family liaison officer would close the relationship with the person or family after they'd supported them through the trauma and helped them through the trial. But Rosemary and Gary have kept in contact.

'I see Gary now purely as a friend, almost like a brother – a very special one, because of what and who he is,' says Rosemary. 'I'll never stop doing that.'

Gary, too, is glad to keep in contact with Rosemary. Not surprisingly, it has taken considerable time to rebuild his self-confidence after the bombing.

'I could hardly bear to look at myself. I didn't see how other people could. Rosemary never flinched from looking at anything. That was important to me. I had chunks out of the back of my head, my hair was burned off, and I was told it wouldn't grow back. Rosemary would say, "Don't worry, sweetheart. You've got a lovely-shaped skull!"'

Gary thinks being gay has helped in their friendship. 'It always makes it more uncomplicated with an attractive woman. I can also explain how men think, which seems to have helped her.'

When Rosemary's mother was seriously ill, it was to Gary that she turned for support.

'As a police officer, I can cope with whatever I have to deal with,' she explains. 'But this was personal, and I couldn't cope.

I'd ring Gary for a chat, a few kind words – and it was enough to carry on. I get a lot from Gary's strong outlook on life.'

Aware that this could all sound like a mutual-admiration society, Gary adds, 'It's a real warts-and-all friendship. Rosemary's seen me when I was very unsure of myself – but she's seen my strengths too. We'll always be in contact, and there for each other.'

Mrs Pettigrew has seen three centuries in her one hundred and six years, while Miles Tubb is a relative spring chicken at only thirty-eight. And yet they are the closest of friends...

An Easy Friendship
Miles Tubb, 2000

It's a rare friendship between Miles and Mrs Pettigrew (who doesn't go in for first names). They first met through Miles's work on the local oral-history project a year ago, and have remained firm friends.

'We talk about everything: politics, snooker – she's a huge Stephen Hendry fan,' says Miles.

'I don't tell him about my courting years, though!' Mrs Pettigrew responds.

Miles is fascinated by the span of Mrs Pettigrew's life.

'Her earliest memory is when she was four, around 1897; her first child was born in 1914; and her first husband died in 1923. It's just the sheer dates!'

Mrs Pettigrew's last surviving daughter of three is currently celebrating her eightieth birthday, and her two nephews are aged eighty-six and eighty.

Speaking about the relationship between these two very different people, Mrs Pettigrew's granddaughter says, 'A lot of people deal with Granny in a very patronizing way. He doesn't, even though he's the youngest person who has come into her life in a long time.'

'We can say anything to each other,' Mrs Pettigrew says. 'I've never met anyone like him. He gave me a new lease on life.'

Miles agrees: 'Me too. It's just a natural easy friendship. It doesn't matter what age someone is – it's whether you get on.'

Bill Thomas wants to thank the stranger who altered his son's life . . .

Strange Meeting
Bill Thomas, 1999

'When my younger son, James, was about twenty he was unemployed, idle and a great source of anxiety to his distracted parents,' Bill says.

At the time Bill was making regular visits to Czechoslovakia, and he decided that he would take James on a trip. This was 1991, and Bill thought that letting him see how people were struggling to survive and progress might inspire James to do something with his life.

'It did open his eyes a bit, but, driving back across Europe, it was clear to me that there was no real change. We stopped for the night at Hanover – only to find that it was the Fair Week, and virtually every room for miles around had been taken. We eventually found a place with just one room, which we had to share. After dinner, we were approached by the only other English person in the place.'

This middle-aged man asked if he could join Bill and James for coffee, and they made small talk.

'Then he asked James how old he was and what he did. Jim

said, "Nothing." "Well," replied our new friend, "it's about time you got off your butt and found a job. The world doesn't owe you a living." Such sentiments had been expressed by his mother and me so many times that I began to take evasive action, waiting for the usual vitriolic response. But, to my surprise, Jim said nothing and went on listening. After about half an hour I went off to bed.

'Next day, the chap had left before us, and James and I made our way through Holland to the ferry. Jim said that he had stayed up for hours talking to the stranger, and found what he had had to say most interesting.'

That trip was a turning point in James's life. When he got home he made enquiries about an access course, went to a university, and got a degree. Now, aged thirty, he runs his own business.

'I often wish', Bill says, 'that I could thank that stranger. He achieved more in an evening than the whole family had in five years. If you believe in angels, that salesman on duty in Hanover certainly fits the specification.'

What can be stranger than magic? Not black, not white, but just straightforward 'Pick a card anywhere from the pack' conjuring-trick-type magic. At just sixteen years old James Tetlow is an accomplished young magician and a member of the Young Magician's Club. His mentor and friend is Graham Mitchell, professional magician and comedian – and also James's teacher.

Magician
James Tetlow, 2005

James recently had his very first professional engagement as a magician – at a dinner dance in aid of MENCAP, where he wowed the diners with his close-up magic and sleight of hand. Perhaps there's nothing too extraordinary in that, but it was something that James's proud parents had never ever expected to see, as James has Down's syndrome.

Ever since he first encountered magic at a party, aged eleven, James has been intrigued by it, to the extent that his parents introduced him to Graham, and the end result was – well – magic.

James and Graham have been mates for five and a half years now, with James studying magic seriously all that time.

'He's doing really, really well,' Graham says. 'And considering he couldn't hold a deck of cards properly, let alone shuffle them, I'm very, very proud of his magic. He's realised at quite a young age that magic is a performing art, and it's all about entertaining.'

It all began at the Watford Association of Magicians' annual fish-and-chip supper. James and his family were invited along, and that's when he experienced close-up magic at first hand. James was completely hooked on it, and that was when he also first met Graham.

Michelle Tetlow, James's mum, is thrilled at the release magic has been for James. 'Every person needs their own forum to excel, and for James some things are harder for him to achieve. Magic was an area where, because he was doing things with his hands and he could see cause and effect, he was able to immediately get something from it and he was able to pass something to other people.'

Graham, however, didn't see a Down's syndrome sufferer when he met James. He knew nothing about Down's and wasn't trained in special needs, so all he saw was a boy with an avid fascination with magic, and that love and fascination inspired Graham in turn.

'As much as people say what I've done for him, he's done so much more for me. James has given me probably the gift of patience, because he has to remember things in a different way,' Graham explains.

The early challenges for James were mostly centred on his mobility, as he had to learn so many new movements. Magic is very technical, and the dexterity required to perform so many of the tricks was a real test of James's commitment and character. But James loves to make people happy, because he's such a happy person himself.

'Everywhere James goes he carries his cards,' Michelle explains. 'In the back of a car, waiting anywhere, on the way to school – he'll be doing his tricks. And because he's doing that people are interested, and it naturally draws an audience and that gives him a forum and a way of actually making new friends, which has been great.'

Graham takes up the story, describing a wonderful night in James's life on holiday one year. 'James performed in a night-club in Kos, when he was away with his family on holiday. It was a talent night. I was fortunate to see a copy of the DVD, and to be honest I was choked, I was so proud of him. Not only did he perform the opening act and do some classics of magic in front of I think it was about 350 people, he was so good they actually asked him to do another two performances: all different magic – linking rings/ropes, cards.'

James always looks smart. Even when he's working on the basics of a routine he will have a smart shirt and trousers on. And he likes to perform to the strains of Bond composer John Barry – 'The name's Tetlow, James Tetlow.'

James is a member of the Young Magicians' Club at the Magic Circle. His ambition over the next two years, besides more performance, is to work towards doing his entry exam for the Magic Circle itself at eighteen. He's a regular attendee at the Young Magicians' Club, and his presence is hugely felt – as a very talented magician, but also as a friend who can be supportive and critical in ways his peers genuinely appreciate.

So much so, in fact, that he was awarded the YMC Member of the Year Award.

'Absolutely fantastic, what a wonderful way to end the day,' Graham says, his voice trembling. 'I was choked. I had tears in my eyes.'

James Tetlow – magician, entertainer, and a young man who makes his friends feel very proud to know him.

The scene is Tottenham, north London. Tony Collins acquired a car – as you so easily can in north London even today – by other than the conventional means of buying one. This was, to be fair to Tony, who now lives in Cornwall, a toy car. And the irregular acquisition of it haunted him for decades.

A Debt Repaid
Tony Collins, 2004

Fifty-five years ago, when Tony was ten, he was mucking about in class because, as he freely admits, he tended to be a bit of an idler. The bell rang for playtime, and as the children were filing out into the playground he spotted this nice little model car. 'And I thought, "Oh, there's a lovely-looking streamlined-looking job there." And it didn't seem to belong to anybody, so I thought, "Well, that can belong to me." So I picked it up.'

Possession being nine-tenths of the law, and all that, it would seem a perfectly reasonable thing to do.

'And I fiddled around with it during playtime, and of course I fiddled around with it after playtime, when we got back to class,' Tony continues. 'And it wasn't long before the eagle-eyed teacher – a lovely chap: Bunny Warren – caught me doing it and said, "Put that away or I'll take it off you." And he took it off me.

'And a hand went up from another side of the class saying, "That's my car." And I said, "No it isn't, it's mine" – lying through my teeth. And the teacher said, "Well, whose is it? Is it yours?" And I said – "Yes." And he said, "Well, where did you get it?" And I said, "My mummy bought if for me." So he said, "Well, all right, I'm taking it anyway." End of school came and he sidled up to me and slipped it back to me – he said, "There's your car back." "Oh, thank you very much." Ever since then I've had this guilty conscience, because I thought, "Well, it did belong to this other chap."'

The other chap in question was one Michael Youens. He was either a mathematical genius or jolly good at sums – the mists of time play tricks with the memory – and Tony wasn't. Michael was also good at sport, and Tony wasn't. You can see where this is going, because Michael – smart alec that he was – clearly *deserved* to have his toy car stolen. Bet that wiped the smug smile off of his face!

'Well, that was my sort of theory at the time really, yeah,' Tony concedes. 'But aside from that he was a really nice – genuine nice – guy. I think everybody loved Michael. He was a great guy.'

Ah.

'Of course, I never took that car back to school again.'

Of course.

The object of Tony's affection – and some of you may be too young or of the wrong gender to appreciate this – was a Dinky model of a Thunderbolt, green, with a fin at the end. It was driven by Captain George E. Eyston, who took the land speed record three times in 1938 – in the real car not the toy – in a neck and neck race with John Cobb.

'And so I kept it pretty quiet,' Tony says, stating the obvious. 'And it preyed on my mind all these years, and I thought, "Well, before I die I've got to right this wrong." And with the help of Friends Reunited I managed to locate this chap, who I hadn't seen since we left junior school. I found out he lived in Shrewsbury. Meanwhile I've lived in Cornwall for the last thirty-five years, so we weren't exactly neighbours.'

Not that Tony could actually return the car. That, like lots of small boys' toys disappeared – lost, or given away by an interfering parent determined to tidy up all that clutter. 'Doing a search on the internet, I found other people had models of this very car for sale – none of them green unfortunately, but the nearest one was blue. So I did a bid for it and won it.'

Moreover, Tony's winning bid was just £6. Some of these vintage toys are now so rare they sell for nearer a thousand. So perhaps, the gods were smiling on him in his quest to put matters right.

Now, toy in hand, Tony could begin his odyssey to Shrewsbury – a bit like Jason and the Argonauts, but in reverse.

'Well, every year I tow a caravan for a tour of Great Britain . . .'

Well, maybe not quite like Jason then.

'I'm one of the pariahs of society – I smoke, own a dog, and tow a caravan. I mean, there's nobody as reviled as I am. Coincidentally, my tour this year was up to the Peak District, and it glanced pretty close to Shrewsbury on my way up there. So I went with this little car in my hand and I knocked on his door, and of course we hadn't been in contact for all these years.'

Tony just turned up – to make it a big surprise for Michael. But Michael's wife answered the door. Michael wasn't in. In fact Michael wouldn't be home till nearly ten that night. And Mrs Youens – who knew nothing of the car theft all those years ago – thought she was sitting opposite a complete loony.

'She looked at me very suspiciously – a strange man knocking at the door in the evening. But I explained it all, and she said, "I tell you what I'll do: give him a ring when he gets back, and I'll hide the car and I won't tell him you've called." Of course that was very obliging of her. So I did that – I phoned him in the evening, and he didn't know me. He didn't remember the episode at all. I suppose in his mind it was a trivial, fleeting thing – he just had a car once, and it went.'

In other words, while Tony had brooded over the car for all those years, Michael had just got on with his life and completely forgotten about it. This was a surprise for Tony.

'Well, this is the thing,' he explains. 'I thought the joy derived from playing with a toy, plus compound interest over fifty-five years – I mean, it would be delirious, wouldn't it?'

Delirium was little apparent at the handing-over ceremony – a moment captured on film by Michael's son. Bemusement was more the overriding emotion on display, apparently.

Nevertheless, Tony felt he'd righted a wrong, and the two men got to chatting about old times, classmates and the teachers, and a bond began to emerge that probably hadn't existed when they were actually in the same classroom. And, whether or not Tony's skirting by Shrewsbury on his caravan tour, they plan to keep in touch.

Next another story of friendship with unusual beginnings – although somewhat more dramatic than a stolen Dinky toy. In 1996 Michael Short's wife, Lillian, died suddenly. Jim Hill became the recipient of one of her kidneys. Two years later, Jim and Michael met.

An Unusual Friendship
Michael Short, 1999

Michael was at Mass when he heard that his wife, Lilly, had collapsed at a football match. He got to the hospital to find her in a very serious condition, and she died a couple of days later.

It was Michael's eldest daughter who asked her father whether he'd thought of donating Lilly's organs. He'd never thought about it, and wasn't very keen on the idea at all.

'It seemed totally alien to me,' he recalls.

But, after speaking to the doctor, and to the organ transplant co-ordinator, Michael and his daughters decided to go ahead.

Meanwhile Jim Hill was suffering from kidney failure and was waiting for a transplant. He didn't have too long to wait before a suitable match was found. After the operation, Jim wanted to meet the donor's family, but he realized that not too many families wish to meet the recipient.

Soon after Lillian's funeral, Michael attended a memorial service in Newcastle Cathedral for families of those who had donated organs and the recipients and their families. It was a sad occasion for Michael. But, at the same time as it brought back memories of Lillian, it also reminded him how she had helped someone live, and this, understandably, brought him some comfort.

'They call it the circle of life,' he says.

Although they had not met, Jim wrote to thank Michael for making his own transplant possible. A correspondence began, with Michael sending Jim a photograph of Lilly and telling him about the kind of person she was. Jim wanted to meet, but for Michael it was still too close to his wife's death, and he didn't feel emotionally strong enough for that.

'When I wrote the letter,' Michael says, 'I explained to him about the lovely service in Newcastle Cathedral which they have every two years. I said the time might be right to meet in about two years. And I did really want to meet Jim.'

So, in the winter of 1998, Michael and Jim arranged to meet. It was an emotional experience for both of them. The ice was broken as Jim and Michael chatted about their families.

'I think Michael probably got a bit of a shock that Lillian's kidney had gone to a Manchester United supporter!' said Jim.

Michael recalled that 'Lilly used to work in a betting shop, and I think Jim likes a bet. It's a funny thing, Jim said, "I seem to get this twitch when I go into a betting shop," and I said, "Ah well, Lilly never liked paying money out."'

10

Beyond Belief

Home Truths was perhaps most famous for stories that made listeners gradually stop what they were doing on a Saturday morning as they became transfixed by the very human tales coming out of their radios. Emotional connections were made and discussion topics for the weekend were created as listeners tried to imagine how they would have coped with the hand that contributors had been dealt.

In the late 1980s Richard Dunn was working as a scaffolder on a North Sea oil rig, sending his money to his wife, Janet, and his three kids back home in Scarborough. He knew his job inside out, and was very safety-conscious. But then just before Christmas 1989 there was an accident . . .

Knock Out
Richard Dunn, 2005

Richard recalls the night it happened: 'I was a night-shift foreman and I was checking a job that the day shift had done when it collapsed on me – the scaffolding itself – and I fell forty foot on to a big steel floor and I shattered both my legs and the bottom of my spine.'

Fortunately, if that word can be used in this context, Richard had considerable experience and knowledge of how to fall from his days in the army. As soon as the scaffolding gave way he pulled himself into the parachuting position, which probably saved his life.

He was flown back to Aberdeen, and underwent a painful, nine-hour operation, followed by some dreadful news.

'The first thing the doctor said to me next morning was, "That's your working days and your walking days over." Well, I'm quite blunt, so I told him to go away – you know ...' Richard has never been someone to be told he couldn't or wouldn't be able to do something.

He was alone when he received the news – his wife was still making her way to Aberdeen from Scarborough – but Janet was the emotional crutch on which he built his recovery, initially visiting him in hospital – when he was moved home – two or three times a day and keeping up his morale. Amazingly, and wonderfully, Richard wasn't the only member of his family in the Scarborough hospital – his youngest daughter was upstairs giving birth to his granddaughter Abigail.

'It was fantastic, absolutely fantastic,' Richard remembers. 'Abigail they call her. She's beautiful. She's fifteen now.'

It was fantastic, it turns out, in ways that Richard couldn't have imagined at the time, as Abigail went on to play a key part in his recuperation.

'I think she was either thirteen or fourteen months old,' Richard explains. 'She was in the back garden on the duvet, and I was sat in my wheelchair watching her while the rest of the family were making some barbecue sandwiches inside, you know what I mean. She stood up and started walking, and I was petrified, so I grabbed my sticks and jumped up at the same time and walked towards her, and she walked towards me, and – bingo! – that were it. So we started walking together. And we're still walking together even now, now all these years later.'

Richard and his granddaughter were taking their first footsteps together, and while she couldn't have known what she was doing, Richard wasn't aware of what he was doing either.

'I just jumped up, you know, and I thought, "Oh Christ, what am I doing?" And that was one of the greatest days of my life when I stood up and started walking again. I'd tried everything to get up on my sticks and I kept falling down, and our lass would pick me up and I'd try again, because I must have been a sod, you know what I mean. But it were a great, great feeling.'

Richard, as you can see, is a fighter, and always has been. He's a big guy, at six foot three, and when he joined the army they took one look at him and stuck him in the boxing ring – a sport he continued with when he left, turning professional in 1969. Those of you who are fans of the sport will know what's coming next, but for readers who couldn't tell a bantamweight from a middleweight let's drag the story out a bit.

Richard turned professional as a way of bringing money into the house – he was married with a young family by then – and he flourished, becoming British and Commonwealth Heavyweight Champion in September 1975. And this, in turn, led to the biggest fight of Richard's career, in May 1976. The venue was Munich, and the opponent was only the greatest boxer of all time . . .

'The greatest of all, yeah, you're right,' Richard agrees. 'The greatest fighter ever lived is Muhammad Ali. It was an absolutely fantastic experience – I loved every minute of it. Like it only comes once in a lifetime for people like me, and I tried to take it with both hands, so I trained as hard as I've ever trained in my life. I'd earned my place to be there, so I were all ready for it.'

Richard remembers the night as if it were yesterday. 'Well, the first round were a bit cagey. I went out like a bull as usual, trying to stick it on him, you know what I mean. But I didn't, obviously, because he was on his toes dancing about and jabbing and flicking me these little punches and talking all the time. You know, "Come on, boy, you've got to work hard to take my title." And . . . well, I can't repeat what I were saying back, because it isn't very nice. But I'm a big blunt Yorkshire man, you see. And the second round were the same, you know what I mean. But the third I cut him with a beautiful right hook and left hook. But after that everything went AWOL. He just opened up on me in the fourth round, gave me a good hiding, and the fifth round that were it – stopped me. I'd been down five times, but I got up five times.'

Richard retired a year after that fight, in 1977, moved to Scarborough, and took up scaffolding – after all, he still had a wife and three children to support. Still, it must have been a strange experience, hoicking scaffolding around after fighting Muhammad Ali.

'No,' Richard disagrees. 'Because the day after I won the British Commonwealth fight I was back at work the next day. And the day I won the European fight I were back at work the next day. That's the way to keep your feet firmly on the ground – you're just one of the lads, aren't you?'

Nonetheless, Ali said some prophetic words that night: 'That Dunn is a tough nut to contend with.' Well, that doctor back in Aberdeen will bear that assertion out, and so will Richard's family.

When he was told he wouldn't walk again, it was a bit like getting up off the canvas with the ref counting him out. 'You think, "I'm not having that,"' Richard explains. 'I just throw it away to one side – it's not going to affect me, I'm going to get on with my life. And that's what I tried to do, and that's what I'm hoping I've done so far. I struggle some days, but you've got to keep at it. You've got to – well, you've got to grit your teeth and get on with it. And that's how I look at life.'

Richard recently turned sixty and one of his most treasured presents was a copy of *The Greatest Fights of All Time*, sent and with an inscription by Muhammad Ali. They'd met a couple of times after the fight, but not since 1985. And that wasn't all. There was an unusual ad in the *Scarborough Evening News* . . .

'He said he'd like a return. I said, "You've got to be kidding at my age," – I'm sixty for heaven's sake. I'm sure he put it in for a bit of fun, like, but it were great.'

Ali never forgot Richard Dunn, and after hearing his story it's easy to see why.

Kenny Richey's story has regularly made the news, ever since he was convicted of the aggravated murder by arson of a two-year-old girl eighteen years ago, in Ohio.

The prosecution claimed Kenny had climbed up to the window of his former girlfriend's flat, thrown petrol through the window, and set the flat alight, killing her daughter, who slept inside. Evidence that the little girl had a history of starting fires and that petrol was not involved in the fire did not come to light during the trial. Kenny's case was reviewed by a federal appeal court in 2003, but he still awaits their ruling.

Cruel and unusual punishment you might think. But under American law, although this new evidence appears to have been accepted by the state, the fact that the case was conducted according to established legal processes means that Kenny can still be executed.

Amnesty International has described Kenny's as a most compelling case of innocence on death row, and more than a hundred MPs have backed his appeal. Kenny certainly needed the support of Karen Torley of Glasgow. The pair had been in contact for nine years, with Karen at first featuring as an ally and friend, and then as Kenny's fiancée. Today Kenny remains on death row, still appealing his innocence.

He and Karen are no longer engaged. Still, if you're curious as to what sort of person gets involved in this way with someone under sentence of death – well, this sort of person . . .

Death-Row Romance
Karen Torley, 2004

Karen, a mother of four, with three grandchildren, first became aware of Kenny in 1992. Because of his Scottish birth, his story had regularly made the news, but Karen had paid little attention to it. Then, in 1995, an Englishman called Nicholas Lee Ingram was executed in Georgia. This time Karen did pay attention, and was appalled at the brutality of electrocution and determined to find a way to fight execution and to help the men on death row.

It was then that she started to read about Kenny's case. 'And the thing that struck me most was the fact that the carpet from the fire had been taken and put in the village dump. You know, they'd kept the carpet in a shed for seventeen days, then rolled it out in front of the police petrol pumps and cut four samples and said there were traces of petrol.' And the petrol was one of the pieces of evidence that helped damn Kenny Richey. Karen started writing to him in 1995, asking him if there was anything she could do to help. 'And Kenny asked me to write some letters to the Supreme Court and the Putnam County Court of Common Pleas, asking that he have a new trial. And basically it just went on from there.'

At the same time as she was writing in defence of Kenny, Karen was also writing to him, with news of her family, what the children were up to, how she'd failed her driving test. After two years of correspondence back and forth, Karen realized her feelings had deepened.

'I thought it was insane, and I thought it was . . . He was going to die, so this was just going to lead to hurt and pain. It was something that I should probably not be doing.'

After a year and a half, Kenny and Karen talked on the phone – although the first time they spoke he didn't understand a thing she said. 'He's Edinburgh, I'm Glasgow, and we've two totally different accents.' And never the twain shall meet. Except that they did.

'I was very nervous about meeting him. The first time that I did actually meet him I felt sick, because the place is not very nice to visit – it's a horrible place. When we met, it didn't seem like meeting a stranger. I thought it would, but it didn't.'

Karen thinks the reason the two of them clicked was a shared sense of humour, though how Kenny can maintain his given the situation he's in is amazing. But perhaps it's the only thing that keeps him going.

However, he probably didn't expect to make Karen laugh when he asked her to marry him. But that was the response he got.

'I started to laugh, because I thought he was doing one of his wind-ups on me – because he does that a lot. And then he started to talk, and I realized that . . . no, hold on a minute, this isn't a wind-up.'

The news of their engagement came as quite a surprise to Karen's family.

'At first my parents were very . . . like most parents probably, they were worried that I was going to be hurt. But my parents have been very, very supportive. And they've spoken to Kenny.'

Her children have been very accepting of Karen's campaigning from day one, and were equally unruffled at her news.

At the time of broadcasting, Kenny is waiting on the Six

Circuit Federal Court of Appeals, where he had a hearing on 7 May 2003, to make a decision on his appeal. While Karen was optimistic, she had to recognize the possibility that, unlike most engaged couples, she might not get to plan for the future. Her and Kenny's future might end at any time.

'Every year you say, "Well, he'll be home by Christmas," and it's now looking extremely unlikely that he's going to be home this Christmas, despite what we did think,' Karen explains. 'So we just have to take it each day as it comes. It's not something that you can dwell on too much.'

Nevertheless, during their daily phone calls they do think ahead and talk about a life together.

'He talks about what kind of house he would like, and he's going to go travelling round Scotland in a caravan thing. He's actually talked about helping other people who are on . . . you know, injustices. He talks about going back to Edinburgh, obviously, which is a bone of contention.'

Kenny also pretends to support Rangers – Karen is a Celtic fan – just to wind her up. Wind-ups are very important to Kenny and Karen.

Kenny gets just one hour of what is styled recreation – time out of his cell – each day. During one of these hours he called *Home Truths*, and described his life in the penitentiary and the impact of Karen on his life.

Initially he thought she was just another do-gooder whose letters punctuate the dull repetition of the days – one of those women who develop strange attachments to prisoners or who want a penpal.

As Kenny talked, a recorded voice cut across the line: 'This call is originating from an Ohio correctional institution and may be recorded or monitored.'

Being regularly interrupted like that is part of the experience of being a prisoner, as well as being listened to.

'It gets annoying, you know,' Kenny admits with wry

understatement. 'They keep interrupting the call. You got calls coming from this institution, like they don't know where I'm calling from, then you've got sixty seconds left, then finally you've got ten seconds left, and then they tell you where it's coming from again and take lumps out of the whole ten seconds.'

When he's not on the phone to Karen, Kenny plays cards in his recreational hour – he's had no physical exercise in years. Kenny's fellow inmates would rather he was on the phone than playing cards, though – not because he beats them, but because they love Karen's Scottish accent.

'This call is originating from an Ohio correctional institution and may be recorded or monitored.'

'Really? Is that right?' Kenny asks, ironically.

Kenny was understandably nervous about making his first call to Karen – and not just because of the exigencies of doing so. She had become such an important feature in his life. He was even more uptight when they finally met for the first time. But he needn't have been. They clicked immediately, and had a grand time. In fact Kenny was smitten the first time he set eyes on Karen, and determined to ask her to marry him – an impossibly romantic gesture given his circumstances.

'Cannae help it – it's in the genes,' Kenny says. 'All Scots are romantic.'

'This call is originating from an Ohio correctional institution and may be recorded or monitored.'

His relationship with Karen is all the more acutely felt because it's hard to make friends on death row, for grimly obvious reasons.

'Oh, it's hard for anybody to lose a mate, you know, especially when they've . . .'

'This call is originating from an Ohio correctional institution and may be recorded or monitored.'

'I think about the future,' Kenny concedes. 'Mostly I stay in the past, because it's pretty much all I've got. But I do think about the future, and what I'm planning to do when I get out and how things might be.'

Back in the present, *Home Truths* then left what remained of Kenny's call to Karen and him.

'What took you so long?' Kenny asks, laughing.

'You're a cheeky swine,' Karen says.

'You have sixty seconds left on this call.'

'OK. I cannae help it, though. I'm just joshing you.'

'We know.'

'You have ten seconds left on this call.'

'Thank God you didn't . . .'

But Kenny's last sentence is interrupted, just like so many of his previous ones:

'This call is originating from an Ohio correctional institution and may be recorded or . . .'

'That's it,' Karen says, as the line goes dead.

It didn't take too many of the real-life stories on Home Truths *each week to remind us just how cruel life has been well within living memory for a great number of people in this country. Even – well perhaps especially – for children.*

Evacuee and Criminal
Dick Pooley, 2005

Dick Pooley was just eleven in 1940 when he and his younger brothers – Tommy, aged seven, and Charlie, aged five – were evacuated from their loving family home in London to a life of Dickensian harshness in Torquay at the hands of one Ma Crocker. The experience was to profoundly affect the course of his life.

The story began with Dick, his brothers and several hundred other children in a school hall, waiting for people to come in and take away the children they wanted. At the end of the process Dick, his brothers and a friend were left. No one wanted them. The boys were put into a hotel for ten days, and then a home was found for them with an old woman – Ma Crocker.

'The experience was a really terrible experience,' Dick tells us. 'We were always hungry. He used to go down on the quay during the summer, which was okay, come back of a night, and had to go straight to bed. But when the winter came we used to sit in the outside toilet. Me and John, the lad who lived in the flats in London under my mother, used to sit on the toilet, and my two brothers would sit on our lap. We'd put our coats around our legs to try and keep them warm, and we had a bit of string that we used to keep the door closed with, and we'd have to wait there until she came home, which would be . . . it would be dark. And then she'd call the cat in, called Smoky – she'd call, "Smoky, Smoky" – and the cat would miaow and go through the door, and then she'd let us in and we'd have to go to bed.'

The boys could never get enough to eat, were always hungry and cold – it sounds like something out of a Dickens novel.

'Cold and hungry, yeah. And it started me off stealing food. My mother, when we left London, she said to me, "Dick, look after the two young lads." And I promised my mother that I would look after them. We were in bed one night, and the two boys said, "We're hungry and we're thirsty." So I went downstairs and filled a milk bowl and I cut a piece of bread and a piece of cheese and took it up to the bedroom. And when she came home she saw that the bread had been cut and the cheese had been cut and she gave us a good thrashing.'

It wasn't as if Ma Crocker wasn't paid to look after the lads, but she always moaned that it wasn't enough. Dick ended up getting a job as an errand boy, pedalling a bike all around Torquay, taking eggs to the hotels. With his earnings, Dick would take the other boys to the cinema – somewhere they could keep warm. He kept the spare money in a Punch and Judy box, until Ma Crocker discovered and took it. Dick was saving for train tickets to get all of them back home to London and their mum. From that point on he started stealing food, and then it escalated to the point where he would steal whatever he could whenever he could.

'We'd always known a loving family, a loving father and mother, and eventually I got caught stealing and Ma Crocker went to court and she gave me a terrible name and said that I was a terrible person. I wasn't. I was a caring person who looked after my two brothers. In the end they put me away for three years in an approved school.'

The school put Dick on the straight and narrow, and when he returned home, aside from calling his mother and father 'Miss' and 'Sir' – much to their amusement – he found a job and kept out of trouble for two years. Until one night at the New Cross Palais de Dance.

'I was with some friends, and I picked up what I thought was my rain mac. And by the time I got to the bottom to go out I was arrested for stealing a mac and the magistrate put me away for a week in Wormwood Scrubs. And after that I was at it for years and years, and landed up with about forty-three years in sentences and I served twenty years in jail. And in Dartmoor I was made one of the first 138 "A" men, which says that I was one of the most dangerous men in Britain.'

All from one week in the Scrubs. The irony was that Dick appealed his prosecution for stealing the coat and was found not guilty, so it never needed to happen. But Dick was seventeen by then and bitter at what had happened to him, and set out on a life of crime.

'I used to blow the safes open, and when I got my last ten years the judge said, "There is no doubt in this court's mind that this man Pooley is one of the top safe blowers in this country and as such the public needs to be protected."'

Dick's life changed when he went to Hull Prison. There he joined a social-studies group run by the chairman of Northern Dairies, Alex Horsley, who brought a wonderful variety of people to the jail to talk to the prisoners. One of them was a publisher, and he and Dick became friends.

'He said to me, "What's a man like you doing in prison, Dick?" I said, "Well, it's funny you should me ask me, George," I said – "I don't know." I said, "I can't answer that." "Well," he said, "I tell you what: I'm going to see that you never go back." And I never did. He got me a job, got me a place to live, published my book, and became my special friend. And it was really down to this man that changed my life.'

Then, a couple of years after leaving prison, Dick went to Hull University to give a talk on prisons to the Applied Social Studies Group, and this changed his life in another, unexpected, way.

'They used to send me a letter and say, "Could you come up to do a talk?" I used to go there – to the office – and confirm that I would be there on such and such a date, and there was an elderly woman who was the secretary. And I went in this particular day, opened the door, and I saw a lovely young girl sitting at a typewriter and I said, "I'm sorry, I thought this was Warren Fox's secretary's office," and walked out. And she said, "I am Warren Fox's secretary." So I went back in, and she was a beautiful-looking girl and she couldn't get rid of me. I asked her would she like to come out and have lunch with me, and she did, and we landed up together.'

Eventually they married, and opened three hostels for the types of ex-convict that no one else wanted to help – murderers, rapists, child-molesters and thieves – and they have been helping these men for over thirty years.

'She came from a sheltered home,' Dick explains about his wife's background. 'She lived in Beverley, her father was a shopkeeper, and they were appalled when they found that their twenty-one-year-old daughter had got herself yoked up with a forty-five-year-old ex-convict. But we've been together now for thirty years, and we've had three lovely boys – good boys, who phone me often. They kiss me when we meet, and they say, "I love you, Dad" and "I love you, Mum."'

Dick Pooley's life has been marked by extraordinary cruelty, terrible mischance and great love. And his only regret? Getting caught – and not even that really, because if he hadn't gone to prison he wouldn't have had the life he eventually had: the opportunities, the friends and, most important of all, the family.

Are you a glass-half-empty or glass-half-full sort of person? Nick Walker is very much a glass-half-full type of man.

Man and Machine

Nick Walker, 1998

'I fancy myself as Peter Fonda in *Easy Rider* – knuckles clenched round handlebars, fists punching the air along the freedom of the highway. King of the Road! Captain America!' Nick Walker says, talking enthusiastically about his love of his scooter.

'I look good: sunglasses, open shirt, trainers, no socks, shoelaces undone – too fiddly. I'm every young man's envy – or at least every young man under the age of five!'

Nick, the engine between his legs, isn't – despite what you might think – hurtling down the open road.

'Scooting through the supermarket, I'm followed by a wake of cries. "Mum, look – the man." And certainly to a child I am a man. But I'm twenty-seven, and it's rare to see someone of that age on a scooter.'

Some of the mothers look away; others look twice. Some even ask Nick questions: 'What did you do? Did you have an accident?' Electric scooters are familiar now on pavements, in supermarkets, parked outside pubs. But they are the property of the elderly. Nick has a friend whose grandfather refuses to use a pavement scooter as he doesn't want to look like an old man!

Nick has no such qualms.

'What brought us together – man and machine – was a mechanical failure of sorts. My wiring started to fail. The complex of nerves which strings my body together began to disintegrate,' he explains. 'I was diagnosed with multiple sclerosis when I was twenty-four. Now the sparks that drive my legs hesitate and falter, and instead I rely on the wiring of this machine.

'A friend of mine once said that we love the members of our family the way we love our limbs. When you lose the ability to use your legs, it is like losing someone you love. What then replaces them itself becomes the object of affection. And I have found love again – I'm in love with my scooter!'

It's tough love, however. Nick rides his scooter hard, as if he were opening the throttle on Route 66.

'I have wrapped my scooter around a lamppost. I hurt the thing I loved,' he says. 'I am more careful now, I am learning. I am making the effort to show I care. And I do really care. It is better, I tell myself, to have loved and lost, and learned to love again, than never to have lost at all. I'm a lucky man.'

Back in 1994 Cathy was pursuing a successful career working as a doctor in A&E. She was happily married to Phil, and they had four children, aged between five and eleven. Then quite suddenly Cathy became ill with severe depression. She was forced to give up work, and spent the next seven years in and out of psychiatric hospitals. Electroconvulsive therapy – ECT – provided some respite, but the effect was only temporary and her condition grew steadily worse.

Depression
Cathy Wield, 2005

To the children she became a shadowy figure, always coming and going, while husband Phil, described by Cathy as a saint, somehow managed to keep the family together – schooled, fed, clothed and stable. Cathy's final cure, if that's the right word, was nothing short of miraculous – her words, but you'd be hard pressed to disagree. We pick up her story some six years ago, at a low point when Cathy was so suicidal that for her own safety the decision was taken to have her sectioned. She was taken, forcibly and against her will, into an ambulance and from there to hospital.

'I was fighting – kicking and screaming – but then realized there was no point: there were two big strong paramedics who'd seen it all before. I got put in the back of the ambulance and unceremoniously taken down to the Royal South Hants Hospital here in Southampton.'

This was, to twist the knife further, the hospital where Cathy worked, a place where the psychiatry department held numerous fears for her – the stories, the stigma. And now she was one of its patients.

'I just remember fear and panic, and all I could do was just go, "Oh God, help me – God, help me," Cathy says. 'And I didn't want to co-operate. In fact I decided that I'd starve myself to death. But they decided that I had to have ECT. And so, even though I didn't consent to it, on this occasion I was given it against my will – which actually wasn't anything like *One Flew Over The Cuckoo's Nest*, because I was so passive anyway they could easily take me and I was anaesthetized. But it started me eating again, and I did get a bit better.'

Even though Cathy was sectioned she was allowed family visits, and her children came to see her regularly, the doctors believing it to be therapeutic for all of them. But the children found it confusing and unsettling. Her son, now nineteen, couldn't understand why the doctors kept taking his mother away but never made her better, and he didn't understand what was actually wrong with her. But he did feel embarrassed, and unable to talk to anyone about it all.

Then the doctors suggested surgery. Now for most people, and certainly for Cathy, this conjured up alarming images from *One Flew Over the Cuckoo's Nest*, but that was far from the reality. And the alternative didn't bear thinking about. The doctors were convinced that, if left untreated, Cathy would successfully commit suicide.

As Cathy explains, modern surgery is a long way away from a lobotomy. 'It's a stereo-tactic technique, which means that they pinpoint a very specialized area in the brain and then they drill a little hole in your head and they insert a probe just to this very specific area and then heat the end of the probe, so it destroys a very small amount of brain tissue in the pathways which are thought to be responsible for this kind of severe resistant depression that I had.'

Cathy – guarded by a nurse on either side – was taken to Dundee, because the Maudsley had closed its unit down, and operated on. When she woke up she felt a sense of resignation. She'd had the surgery that everyone had urged her to have, and she felt no different. Her determination to escape from hospital and kill herself was as strong as ever. And then something startling happened.

'Well, in the few days . . . I mean, I had to recover from the headache and generally was feeling a bit grim, as one does,' Cathy tells us. 'And then on day eight I was sitting with a nurse and another patient came into the room and she just said, "All I want is to be at home with my husband and children." And at that minute I was thinking, "Oh shut up!" But in fact a light switched on in my head, just seemed to fill my head, and I just thought, "That's what I want – all I want is to be at home with my husband and children," and I realised something had changed, that in fact the depression had gone. It just seemed to lift in that instant. Then I was extremely confused, because there I was in a Scottish hospital, five hundred miles from home, with a nurse beside me, on a section, and I thought, "How the heck am I going to get out of this?"' After all, the nurses were trained to recognize the ruses of patients who wanted to slip away and commit suicide.

So Cathy phoned her husband, Phil, and he immediately knew something momentous had happened, and eventually she was able to convince the doctors that she was okay.

'I was absolutely just exuberant after I left – almost danced to the car, just couldn't believe it. I just came into home and wanted to suddenly clear everything up because obviously after seven years away you can imagine . . .'

Seven years away, during which time Cathy's two children had gone from five and eleven to twelve and eighteen – an enormous period in their lives which she had missed out on, and during which they'd had no mother to help them. Now, all of a sudden, she was back.

'Yes. Well, my oldest daughter, Rebecca, had been through the Royal Ballet School and was a ballet dancer, and she actually came from Germany where she was working and visited me in Scotland after I was better, and she was just simply delighted. And all the children were delighted. But then Mum suddenly became Mum and – I've asked Jonathan, the youngest, if I could have his permission to say this – he was quite resentful initially when I started telling him to do things. I'd say, "Go to bed," and you know, who's this woman who's walked in and suddenly taking over?'

'So one day he came home from school and rang the door-bell and I answered the door and he wouldn't come in, and I said, "What's up?" And he said, "Are you ever going back to that hospital?" And I said to him, "No, never." And he just kind of breathed a sigh of relief, walked in, and was no prob-lem from that time on.'

Cathy had become a mum again, but she also had to become a wife once more. The neurosurgery programme took a heavy toll on marriages, Cathy reckoned she and Phil were the only couple that stayed together.

'Well, he's nothing but an angel, I think. He's been absolutely amazing. And of course he was absolutely exhausted, and it was a very difficult year for our marriage. We just had to work things through, get to know one another again.'

Seven years is a very long time, and Cathy felt like a latter-day Rip Van Winkle in many aspects of her life, from the serious to the flippant. However, she found discovering this new world – a world with email, for instance – exhilarating and exciting. Still, the threat of the depression returning always lingered.

'Since I've recovered I have had a brief episode where I became a bit depressed after being stressed after returning to work full-time. But I went for help immediately, and got over it very, very quickly. But I acknowledge that I've got a vul-nerability, and I just need to be careful.'

Cathy may feel as if she's been asleep for seven years, but to her family and friends the Cathy they loved has returned, unchanged from the woman they knew before her illness. And for that they're all grateful.

When Tim was in his early twenties his parents died of cancer within three years of each other, without the subject being discussed with, or explained to, Tim and his younger sister. When Tim's wife Julie was diagnosed with breast cancer, ten years ago, Tim was determined that their two daughters would not experience the bewilderment he'd suffered.

Talking about Death
Tim Horne, 2003

'It must have been about seven years ago. Things were not quite right, but we weren't quite sure what, and there were all sorts of tests done, and no one really looked for breast cancer. They came up with all sorts of other ideas,' Tim says, remembering his wife's diagnosis.

One of the doctors' suggestions was mastitis, which soon after the birth of the second child is aggravated by breastfeeding. At that stage Julie was in her early thirties.

'But somehow, possibly because of what I'd been through before, the suspicion kicked in, and I just wondered. On the day that I knew things were really quite serious my ship was headed for Hong Kong and I was flown home to sort things out.'

Home was Sydney, which was where Julie's condition was finally diagnosed.

'And the initial breast-cancer operation was done there – the mastectomy – and then we started the wait to see if it had spread or not.'

Tim, who served in the Royal Navy, was then posted back

to the UK and Plymouth. Soon after their return to Britain, Julie's symptoms returned, with the cancer spreading to her bones. The doctors were positive that new drugs could arrest the disease, giving Julie an extra precious year of life.

However, that year was blighted with excruciating pain, and inevitably Julie's thoughts turned to her death, as she wondered if it was better to die than to continue suffering so much. So Tim and Julie did talk about her death – but always in the context of getting on with life and sorting out the practicalities of life without her. Tim hired a nanny for the girls, and his mother-in-law came from Australia to help out. Moreover, the couple were active churchgoers and felt very well supported by the church and their network of friends; and their faith helped them prepare positively for life after Julie died.

Julie had a number of requests for when she was gone, from the traditional – she wanted her ashes scattered back home in Australia – to the more unusual – she insisted that Tim remarry.

As much as Tim and Julie were open with each other and with friends and family, they were careful how they handled the children. Tim wanted them to understand what was happening to their mother, but they were young – six and four – and he didn't want to distress them unnecessarily.

'Everything sort of fell into place,' Tim says. 'We got to a Sunday, it was clear that Julie had deteriorated, the children and I went to church. I took them to see her afterwards. It was obvious things were going downhill, and at that stage I knew that I needed to make sure they were involved and comprehended, as best they could at that age, what was going on. And, as it happens, on a Sunday a child psychiatrist was made available through the hospital. He and I had a very constructive chat for over an hour, and that's when one has to ask awkward questions like is it better to say "Mum has died" or is it better to say "Mum is going to die" and a bit later say "Mum has died"?'

The psychiatrist's answer was to do both. So Tim went home, gathered his children together, and told them what was going to happen to their mother. When Julie died he took them to see her body – another recommendation of the psychiatrist's.

'It was a matter of putting everything in context, enabling them to comprehend what was going on in their lives, at an age when it was quite difficult. And to enable them to say their goodbyes, and to see that Julie's life had ended, and to move on. So the funeral was very much focused on the children, almost directed at them, so that they understood what was going on. What did throw me a little bit was, having decided that Julie was to be scattered in Australia, I had obviously made arrangements such that the urn would be delivered back to the house, so that I could give it to my in-laws to take with them. But one sort of forgets, so there is a time when there is a knock on the door and there is a man with an urn. Of course the kids – I had explained what was going to happen, and of course one has to take the lid off the urn to let them have a look, because that is the level of interest. It just seemed the right thing to do.'

Tim's daughters have now grown into typical teenagers. They understand what happened to their mother and, unlike Tim confronted by his own parents' silence, have adjusted to their loss, with no recriminations about what Tim did or did not do.

As well as having Julie's ashes scattered back home, Tim has also followed her other command and remarried. Ingrid, his new wife, interestingly, is also his oldest daughter's teacher. The announcement required a bit of tact.

'One had to be very careful, and almost let the children think they had thought of the idea. I hadn't met Ingrid before Julie died, but she was at the funeral because she had gone to represent the school. Anyway, when the time came, it was a matter of "Well, maybe Dad ought to think about getting married at some stage." To which the children said, "Yes, we had thought about that." And I said, "Oh yes, any ideas?" And they said, "Well, how about the nanny?" And I said, "Well, no, she is very nice, but probably not the best for me." And so, "Well, how about Ingrid?" And I said, "Well, yes, there is some thought in that, that is quite a good idea."'

Tim's girls were the bridesmaids at his and Ingrid's wedding, and the four of them have been together for ten years. Julie, however, still remains a real presence in all of their lives, through the girls' grandparents and through their memories. And if the girls ever want to talk about their mother, then that's all right by Tim.

The party-conference season is not nearly as interesting to the rest of us as the participants imagine. But for Edward Berry the conference season brings back painful and poignant memories of a conference in Brighton twenty-two years ago, when something momentous and murderous happened.

The Brighton Bombing
Edward Berry, 2004

It was Friday 12 October 1984, and in the early hours there was a big explosion at the Brighton hotel where the Prime Minister and others attending the Conservative Party conference were staying.

Four people died in that explosion, including Sir Anthony Berry, the former MP for Southgate – a junior minister in

Margaret Thatcher's government and Edward's father. Edward Berry's sister Jo subsequently became news herself when, in order to come to terms with what had happened to their father, she eventually met with Patrick Magee, the man convicted of planting the bomb. But until now Edward has never spoken publicly about the effect his father's death, and the manner of it, had on him.

Edward contacted *Home Truths* and told us he wanted to talk about the day that he described as 'without doubt the most extraordinary day of my life'.

He talked first about having dinner with his father the night before, and realizing that they had become good friends.

'We probably became closer as I got older. You know, the relationship between any adults, as the younger one becomes an adult, has more to it, and you share views and you discuss things. And, yes, you speak on a similar wavelength,' Edward says, recalling that night. 'It was one of those actually really rather special times, and I say that – I like to think – not just with hindsight. I think even if he had lived that evening was quite special, because I had just returned from working in France. I'd been there for a year. I'd got myself a new job – I was feeling pretty excited about that. And he had come through quite a difficult experience. So the two of us were on a sort of a positive note, and we had a very special evening together.'

Edward's father had recently overcome some personal problems and was beginning to feel a lot more positive about the future. A very meticulous man, from a strict background, Sir Anthony had led a blemish-free life until one night in July 1984. Returning from dinner with friends, he got out of his car because there was a jam of some sort ahead. A policeman sorting out the hold-up spotted him and decided that he was probably a little the worse for wear. Sir Anthony panicked, got back in his car, and drove off – but not particularly well. He was done for drink-driving, which for him would be distressing enough. But then in September the story hit the papers.

'And that absolutely devastated him,' Edward remembers, 'despite the fact that later on there was – in the paper – a rather nice cartoon by Jak, the cartoonist, and I have the original.

'Anyway, that happened. And so when we had dinner that night what I saw was a man who'd pulled himself up. And I'd got this new job, and he was very proud of that and was keen to talk about that, so it was just one of those evenings that I treasure because it was so special.'

The night his father died, Edward was staying a mere two blocks away, but he didn't hear the explosion. They'd parted at around eleven thirty, and then the next morning the phone rang. It was one of Edward's sisters asking after their father. He had no idea what she was talking about – he hadn't heard the bomb.

'And I turned on the news, and you could see – this was quite early on, this was six: it had only happened four hours earlier, five hours earlier – there were pictures of the hotel, and they said that people had been moved from the hotel to the Metropole, which is the hotel just adjacent, also facing the front. So I immediately went there. And that was the start of the day really – looking at a sea of faces in a room in a hotel, a huge room, of people covered in dust, people in pyjamas and dressing gowns and nighties, looking dazed, just trying to find a familiar one or two.'

Sir Anthony had been with Edward's stepmother, Sarah – she'd joined them for dinner the previous night. But now he couldn't see either of them. He eventually found the police control centre, where someone told him that Sarah Berry had been taken to the West Sussex County Hospital, but that was all he knew. Edward went to the hospital, where he saw Norman Tebbit and Sarah – who had damaged her pelvis.

'I think this is when it dawned on me: there's a delay, why is there this delay?'

Inevitably, Edward started to fill in the gaps in his imagination. Somehow the day moved in slow motion and yet flew by, there was so much going on. Edward doesn't think of himself having had a particularly remarkable life, but that day was certainly extraordinary. When he talks to his children about that day, it's partly to bring their grandfather to life and partly an attempt to make sense of the day: did something positive come out of it, or was it just a terrible experience?

Edward first suspected his father was dead when he heard that they'd found a body. He began to feel a creeping sense of doom, but tried to keep himself upbeat.

'And we had this strange experience with these dogs. My stepmother was very fond of these two Jack Russell terriers that she had called Lucky and Smudge, who always travelled with her. There aren't many hotels that accept small dogs in the rooms, but she's a very forceful character when it comes to her pets and these two dogs were with her. And I discovered, again through one of my sisters, who had seen one of these dogs on television, that a fireman had taken one of these dogs. And I then heard from the police that the other dog was with the RSPCA, and I said, "There's just something I have to do today, which is to bring the two dogs together" – which happened to be a mother and daughter. And that was probably one of the most moving moments of the whole thing. If you're not a dog lover or whatever, you might think well it's a bit sort of trivial, but just bringing a mother and daughter dog – for one who is completely emotionally washed out – bringing the two dogs together was something that . . . a little moment of joy in this ridiculous day.'

Reuniting the dogs was a useful diversionary tactic, but when Edward returned to the hospital he was asked to identify a body, and he said no, he couldn't do it.

'I don't know whether I made the right decision, but I said no. I said, "I don't think I can." And in fact my final memories, visual memories, of my father are of a man standing tall, as he was very tall, heading off into the distance, so I perhaps prefer those.'

Edward sat and talked to Sarah, feeling phenomenally calm. She was gasping for a glass of wine, so Edward snuck off to the off-licence for a bottle of red, which he promptly dropped on the floor. He had more success with the second one, and the two of them polished it off.

Some years later Edward's sister Jo embarked on a project to meet and be reconciled with Patrick Magee – the man who had planted the bomb.

'I think for a variety of reasons my views on that I sort of keep to myself. I think her heart's in the right place, and if she's doing some good then I can only think that that's a good thing,' Edward says.

But it's not something he would ever do.

'I probably remove it even from the troubles in Northern Ireland,' he goes on – 'just bad luck: wrong place, wrong time. I wouldn't relish meeting them – I don't think we'd put our arms around each other. I think that the people who do these things are committed, and given the chance would do them again. He didn't actually achieve the objective that was set before him, so I suppose I feel that any punishment that is imposed is appropriate. Now obviously he came out part of a much bigger picture, and I would not do anything to stop the potential for peace in any part of the world if there has to be certain sacrifices, and obviously these decisions were made at a very high level. But I'd find it hard to look him in the eye.'

*Can anyone imagine what goes through someone's mind
when they lose a partner through suicide? Perhaps the
overwhelming thought might be, 'If only I'd been there to
listen, to talk, perhaps I could have done something.' It's
because of thoughts like these that you might bump into
Keith Lane, sitting in his car on top of Beachy Head, one of
the most common suicide sites in the country. But he doesn't
go there to brood. He simply goes to provide a last resort, to
be the one person that can save another's life from coming to
a premature end.*

Suicide Watch
Keith Lane, 2005

'We'd been together for seven years – eight years now it would
have been – and we just met in a pub, just Mills & Boon. We
just looked at each other and that was it – we fell in love,
from that moment to the day she died.' Keith Lane, a window
cleaner from Eastbourne, is talking about his wife, Maggie.
'And she was a wonderful woman – absolutely beautiful,
absolutely articulate. She was – oh – the light of my life.'

Maggie told Keith that he wasn't just her best lover as well
as her husband, but was also the best friend she'd ever had.
Someone in whom she could confide anything.

'Although,' he adds, 'there were certain things, obviously,
that were troubling her, and that's why she ended up where
she did in the end. But they were cracks within rather than
any cracks in our relationship, because there weren't any.'

But Maggie was depressed – an illness which had its roots
in her childhood. Depression drove her to drink, which in
turn made her even more depressed. Eventually she tried to
commit suicide.

'She'd tried on five other occasions, four of which were
just a cry for help. She would try and drown herself in the

bath, but she'd leave the window open so I could get in. She did try properly – she took an overdose – but I came back home early from golf, luckily, and I found a suicide note beside the bed saying, "I'm sorry, darling, I love you." She'd taken a lot of tablets, but we rushed her to hospital and we managed to save her on that occasion. But that was the first really serious attempt, and that was the first time she'd ever left a note.'

Maggie didn't leave a note ten days later, when she finally succeeded in taking her life. She had just started a new job. She told Keith she was going into work, and kissed him good-bye as he went off as he always did. At lunchtime she phoned him to say she'd gone home, unhappy with the job, but would go back because she needed the money. Keith could tell she was unhappy, but her tone wasn't unfamiliar.

'I wasn't overly worried,' Keith explained. 'But I did ask her was she OK, and she said, "Yes, fine. Just remember to put the jacket potatoes on and I'll be in at quarter to six. I love you, darling." And they're the last words she ever said to me.'

'She didn't arrive home at quarter to six, but I wasn't unduly worried, because she'd gone missing before. She would normally go to a hotel and check in, and then she'd ring me about midnight and tell me where she was and then I'd have to go and pick her up. So I wasn't unduly worried that she hadn't come in,' Keith continues.

But at about half past nine the police knocked on the door asking Keith if he knew his wife was missing. He said yes, and they told him not to be too alarmed but they'd found her car at Beachy Head. They wanted the spare keys, so they could get inside to see if there were any clues to Maggie's whereabouts. At that point Keith got a little bit worried, because Beachy Head is a very renowned suicide spot.

'They said, "Well, we've got the helicopter looking, but at the moment we can't find her." And it wasn't until about three, three thirty in the morning they came back, only this time they'd driven the car back with them and they brought her handbag with her mobile and her gloves and everything that was inside the car. Now at that point obviously I was now getting really worried, because she wouldn't go out without her handbag and mobile.'

The following morning at first light Keith went up to Beachy Head to search for himself. He hunted for three hours, but to no avail. In fact he probably stopped just short of where Maggie lay.

'I wouldn't have wanted to have seen her down there. But I gave up and went home, and they called on me again about three o'clock in the afternoon. There were two policemen standing on the doorstep, and they take their hats off and you just know there's something dreadfully wrong. And then they just came in and they told me that they had reason to believe that they'd found my wife's body at Beachy Head.'

At that moment Keith's mind went blank.

'You just don't know what to do, so you don't have any emotions other than the pain that you're feeling.'

In the days that followed, Keith asked himself why he didn't go home at lunchtime. Was there something he could have done? Was there something he'd missed?

'Yes, you do feel guilty – you can't help that. It's a natural thing.'

A week after Maggie died, Keith returned to Beachy Head. He hoped it might help him come to terms with what had happened. And then he noticed a woman.

'There was a lady up there and she was writing a note, and I obviously became suspicious and I questioned her as to what she was doing. And it was quite obvious she was writing a suicide note. At which point I cried. And she said, "What are you crying for?" And I said, "Well, my wife went over there last week, and this is all too much." And she said, "In that case you must understand that I have the right to do what I want to do."'

With that the woman threw the paper and pen on the ground and made a run for the edge of the cliff. Keith chased after her, grabbed her, and rugby-tackled her to the ground and held on to her until the police arrived – which was surprisingly quickly, as the woman had been listed as missing and they were looking for her.

The police struggled to get the woman into the police car, so Keith went with her to the police station so that she had company.

'She lay in my arms and cried, and I cried, so it was almost like having my wife in my arms, you know. This is only a week after she's died, for goodness sake, and here I am cradling a woman that I'd just saved,' Keith continues. 'And it was all so surreal. And then I went to the hospital to see her, and she hated me – absolutely hated me – for what I'd done. But I said, "I'm not going to give up on you" and I went about five times to the hospital I suppose, just to prove to her that people out there do care about life, do care about people living. And eventually she began to warm to me. I took pictures of my wife to show her, and we sat in the ward and cried together. Then about three or four months afterwards I was walking through Eastbourne and she tapped me on the shoulder and she said, "You're the man that saved my life, aren't you?" And then I looked round and I said, "How are you?" She said, "What's your name?" And I wouldn't give it. I said, "The most important thing is how are you?" And she said, "I'm fine thank you," she said – "I'm so grateful." And that's what prompted me to do what I do today.'

Keith decided that if someone had been up on Beachy Head when his wife had gone up there then perhaps she would be alive today. And so many people have died up there – thirty-eight last year; twenty-one already this year – that Keith decided that they needed a twenty-four hour watch.

'We won't save everybody, but we will get the numbers drastically down. So I then started to try and organize a charity to try and raise funds.'

Keith goes up every morning and afternoon for an hour's watch at a time. He still has to work, so going for longer is difficult. There's a group called The Chaplains who keep a watch from seven until midnight, but there are fifteen hours when there's no one. Nevertheless, Keith has managed to talk down nine people.

'You don't actually plan anything – it just comes to you,' Keith says, explaining how he approaches the potential suicides. 'Because I'm speaking from the heart, like I am today, you can feel for them. I know the pain, I know the anguish, I've lost somebody there, so you just go up to them and you just explain who you are and you say, "I know how you feel." The normal reaction is "Oh no you don't," but when they learn that you do actually know most of them just want someone to listen to them, because there's nobody out there listening to them – that's what they feel. They feel they're alone. And then suddenly there's this person there talking to them who does know what they're talking about.'

Keith tries to get the people's mobiles off them, take down their numbers, and ring their families. Then he takes them for a drink, talks to them, makes them feel wanted, that life is worth living.

'I say, "I'm proof of that." And maybe that's what touches them, I don't know. All I know is that when I start talking to them they just seem to look me straight in the eye, and once I've got eye contact with them I know that they're not going to jump – I just know they're not. And I'm just so confident that I'm going to get them back and give them a chance.'

Some of the people Keith meets feel like that first woman did: hate turning to gratitude. Some just disappear. Others remain in touch.

'A seventeen-year-old boy that I saved, who came down from Mansfield – he was just up there because he was failing his exams – he's OK now. His girlfriend has phoned to say that he's doing very, very well at college now, so he's fine. It's lovely to hear that these people are alive and are well, but it has a tinge to it, because I think, "Oh God, why wasn't someone there for my wife?"'

Keith Lane earned a bravery award for that first life he saved, and he's a courageous and strong man in many, many ways. But he's probably never had to be braver than when the police arrived on his doorstep that fateful afternoon.

Acknowledgements

Writing and compiling this book would have been impossible but for various people, some obvious and some less so. The presenters who were the glue of the programme, the reporters who teased out some extraordinary stories, and the contributors who gave of themselves for our illumination, education and entertainment are, of course, the obvious candidates. But let's also not forget the Volvo drivers, eccentrics, rabbits and cats in life jackets (my favourite) who inspired some of these stories.

As important were the team at the BBC. Chris Burns and the production department behind *Home Truths* who made the programme week in and week out, and still found time to help me put this book together, producing myriad CDs of stories for me to listen to without a grumble. Stephanie Eason, who transcribed those stories with great dedication, and Edward Faulkner at John Murray, whose editorial insights were telling and adroit, both played an essential part too in what you have read.

But ultimately, however trite this might sound, there's one great vote of thanks that ought to be paid, and that's to the man who simply was *Home Truths*, whose voice and personality brought humour to surprising situations, provided contributors with the room to speak, and never allowed the emotional to become sentimental: John Peel.

Mark McCallum
June 2006

Mark McCallum

Mark McCallum has worked in and around publishing for over twenty years and has co-authored a (reputedly) funny book, *Back to Basics*, as well as writing for various magazines and papers. He works as a marketer for a number of brands, but even more interestingly he once wore Frank Finlay's moustache – about which he's understandably tight-lipped.